P9-BTX-961

$6.95

THE DEVIL'S FRONT PORCH
By Lester Douglas Johnson

Here is a remarkable document—the vivid recollections of a man who for thirty years was an inmate of the Kansas State Penitentiary at Lansing.

To say that the prison at Lansing was bad is hardly necessary. From its founding in 1864 through the decade of the twenties, Lansing was one of the most feared and hated prisons in the country. Men who had survived the ordeal of a sentence there called it the Devil's Front Porch—the nearest thing to hell. The system for handling convicted felons was traditional—"break him or kill him." Most of the prison personnel set about this task with zeal and dedication. An uncommon feature about Mr. Johnson's story is that he has told it with objectivity and with compassion both for his fellow prisoners and for their tormentors.

The book is written from the vantage point of one who is constantly a member of the cast, always on stage but never the star. His story opens at the turn of the century when Lansing still housed some of the outlaws left over from riotous times, and the reader is carried from the days of the buggy to the days of the jet, discovering meanwhile that the earth turns considerably more slowly in the murky world behind prison walls. The roaring twenties produced a bumper crop of well-publicized criminals, and the Devil's Front Porch received its fair share. Some of the more infamous were Alvin (Ole Creepy) Karpis, Freddie Barker (one of "Ma" Barker's versatile sons), Wilbur Underhill (known as the Tri-State Terror), and the inimitable Bill LaTrasse, perhaps one of the most colorful and likeable of them all.

Along with the day-to-day account of life within the prison and the history of the slow march of progress and reform are stories of the prisoners themselves. Sadism, brutality, homosexuality, injustice, and the very air of violence and hopelessness in which convicts exist are all here. There is also a strange nobility, a genuine affection, and sometimes a wry and bitter humor, as when a condemned man approached the gallows, looked it over carefully, and said, "This is sure gonna teach me a lesson."

In this significant and absorbing book, the reader will follow with fascination the history of the prison as it unfolds, and somewhere before the final sentence, he will find himself exploring his own relationships with his fellow-men and questioning the concepts of imprisonment as rehabilitation and capital punishment as a deterrent to crime. Mr. Johnson's book demonstrates that it is our common tragedy that our soaring technology has so outdistanced advances in human relationships and that we know so much of the world we inhabit but so little of ourselves.

THE DEVIL'S FRONT PORCH

By LESTER DOUGLAS JOHNSON

THE UNIVERSITY PRESS OF KANSAS
Lawrence / Manhattan / Wichita / London

THIS BOOK IS AFFECTIONATELY
DEDICATED TO MY MOTHER, WHO
ALWAYS UNDERSTOOD; MY SISTER
GRACE, WHO NEVER DID; AND MY
BROTHER GUY, WHO ACCEPTED ME,
WIN, LOSE, OR DRAW.

Contents

Foreword

I STARTED READING *The Devil's Front Porch* with certain misgivings, a feeling that I was merely exposing myself to another convict book, complete with sadism, brutality, homosexuality, and injustices of many sorts. However accurate the contents might be, I did not anticipate the reading of it as a unique literary experience. My hesitancy was not the result of resistance to unpleasant subjects, nor a lack of sympathy toward the issues. For a number of years I have been associated with various efforts to reform our archaic jail and prison systems, which stand alongside our proud churches, libraries, temples, and other edifices of learning, healing, and inspiration as tragic monuments to the inability of the human race to come to grips with, and successfully change, those members who have not fulfilled the social contract.

Obviously, enough has not been said on the subject. Yet, I had to question whether another book on the practice of barbarisms in our time, even though written by a man with considerable acquaintance with the esoteric prison, was what I wanted to, or find good reason to, read. Concerned with man's inhumanity to man, I found myself wondering if the further delineation of prison cruelties was the best manner of breaking through the immunities which the public mind seems to possess, or whether this in itself prompts such revulsion that most people refuse to think about the problem. It was quite likely, I thought, that articles and books depicting both prisoners and guards as animals prevent the average citizen from relating to these men. If they were identified as creatures without normal feelings and thoughts, many people might turn their attention to other more easily understood persons in need.

I was delighted, then, to discover that Mr. Johnson had given us a book in which the subjects emerge as vital human beings and not ogres. This was not a simple task, because it was necessary for the characters to accomplish their realism in an unreal world, one alien to most persons. This reality was dependent upon the revelation of the emotional and mental struggles in which the participants interact and vent upon one another the results of their frustrations and despair toward a life with which they have failed to cope.

Cruelty is here. It is a brutal world described by Lester Douglas Johnson; but one can only wonder if that was not a world less cruel than the one of today, which has become overwhelmed by the sheer weight of numbers and is yielding to the greater inhumanities of anonymity. The considerable efforts to break down a man's individuality in the prison of fifty, forty, or thirty years ago was at least a recognition of that individuality and perhaps preferable to the stultifying cruelty of uninvolved impersonalization.

Humane prison officials are still generally paying mere lip service to individualized treatment—the new ideal of using each prisoner's hangups and converting society's misfits to crime-free lives. Yet all this usually amounts to what penologist Howard Gill has called "birdshot penology." All the bands, baseball, radios, and choirs cannot gloss the fact that real rehabilitation is rare. Caging far outranks curing. Only two percent of all prison inmates are now being exposed to any kind of reform-oriented innovation. Nothing appears crueler than the promise of something withheld. As Leonard Berkowitz has explained, cruelty from unrealized hopes is greater than from deprivation alone. The deprived person who has no hope cannot really be said to be frustrated, because he does not really have a goal he is trying to move toward. A person works harder to get something—whether it is food, a sexual object, or freedom—if he thinks he has a chance. Similarly, his frustration is most severe when he is blocked from satisfaction that he thinks could be his. In social terms, this concept of frustration reveals itself in revolutions of rising expectations. Poverty-stricken groups are not frustrated merely because they have suffered severe deprivations; they are frustrated when they begin to hope. Privation is far less cruel and less likely to cause violence than is the dashing of hopes.

Violence becomes the bedfellow of frustration when low inhibitions are also present, as they are in *The Devil's Front Porch*. The normal level of inhibitions to violence in our society is not particularly high. We take a lenient attitude toward what is sometimes called defensive aggression. It is quite permissible, even admirable, for a man to defend himself with vigor. Nowhere is violence more consistently and enthusiastically touted than in movies and on television. Violence is often defended on the grounds that it serves as a cathartic. The theory, loosely derived from Aristotle's view of the function of tragedy, contends that violence that is indulged in vicariously drains a reservoir of accumulated hostility and releases tensions that might otherwise explode into actual violent behavior. The theory receives additional support from the ideas and writings of the eminent ethologist Konrad Lorenz. Lorenz stresses the physiological rather than the psychological as a source of behavior: behavior results, he says, from the spontaneous accumulation of some excitation or substance in neural centers. He believes that present-day civilized man suffers from insufficient discharge of his aggressive drive, and he recommends that society provide people with "safe" ways of venting their aggressive urge.

The question is, DO vicarious or real-but-innocuous outlets in fact reduce the chances that aggressive behavior will occur? Although many psychologists continue to subscribe to the catharsis theory in some form, many others believe, and have demonstrated in experiments, that witnessed violence can stimulate actual violence and that a little aggression, like a snowball, can gather momentum and grow.

Once sex used to be the most frightening bogy to haunt the American scene and keep the guardians of public morals and sensibilities on the qui vive; but while American attitudes toward sexual matters seem to be in flux, an equivalent escalation in violence has been greeted by critical confusion, hysterical warnings, and, predictably, big sales in the book stores and long lines at the box office. Precautionary steps against an excessive flaunting of violence in books and on the screen seem absurd in a nation racked by racial tension, increase in violent crime, war, and the ever-present threat of instant annihilation. No less a social observer than General de Gaulle was quoted by Raymond Tournoux in his book *The General's Tragedy* as deploring the fact that since the Kennedy assassination, "America is returning to its old demons."

That old American demon of violence, however, has remained quite present in the public mind through the years, nurtured in part by the movies. American films are a cinema of violence, with the conflict on the screen usually resolved in terms of action. That the film medium was spectacularly apt to shock and overpower its public became immediately apparent when Lumiere's locomotive headed straight for the audience, forcing them to lower their heads and shut their eyes. That same train heralded the arrival of censorship, the means to protect the mass audience from all it did not wish to see or know, anything that would imperil its comfort, physical or psychological.

Yet, off the screens the train continues to charge toward the public; and the message that Mr. Johnson gives us is the repudiation of the catharic value of violence as, at least, it applies to the behavior of those who are the principle perpetrators and, in turn, recipients of violence. Mr. Johnson holds before us the prison wherein men of violence have been treated with, pushed toward, and unprotected from, violence, and have, thereby, become increasingly more violent—violence begetting violence. And the author's thesis is that this evolution is not limited to imprisoned men, but is only more obvious in a setting designed to make of frustration a way of life. The lessons, which apply equally, though perhaps more subtlely, to free men, are unmistakenly there; and they are given voice in the author's plea that we strive for an understanding of violence before it is too late, not only for individuals trapped in its dynamics but for society as a whole. In this he would agree with Bruno Bettelheim who feels that we sow the seeds of delinquency when we fail to acknowledge that aggression is a part of each of us, and that we choose to remain ignorant of its nature rather than learning to cope with it.

Tragedy is here, as is comedy, and their outward display in laughter and tears. But the tragedy is never pure, for the tragedians are not pure; and the real tragedy is aptly described in the comic gestures of men who have lost both the inner and outward control of their lives, acting out their roles in much the same manner as characters in the existentialistic Theatre of the Absurd. Nor can the comedy come off unstained, for the comic situations and responses must remain the bitter fruit of activities in which there is little room for optimism or humor. The imminence of the pathetic so permeates each and every situation that one cannot completely forget that where comedy unfolds, tragedy is not far behind.

It is within the synthesis of the comic and the tragic, rather than in their separation, that the drama unfolds; and the certain knowledge that they are inseparable creates the movement toward a reality in which the destinies of the players are somewhat foreordained and their fates, like those of the characters in the Greek tragedies, are so arrayed against them that changes in their makeup are not likely to occur that will be sufficient to save them from a tragic end. The comedy, where it does exist, comes in the classical sense whereby some are able to emerge from the pergatory in which they have cast themselves to evolve a better world; and when this occurs, there is a brightness which, if not humorous, produces a profound feeling of hope.

This synthesis of tragedy and comedy is necessary in order for the reader to focus on the identities of the characters. They are not revealed merely as marionettes dancing to the tunes written for them by unloving composers. Their own involvement and their contributions to their sad situations retrieve them from being victims of forces entirely beyond their control. Because of this, of course, they cannot be allowed the sympathy afforded the small child struck down by paralysis, or the father who loses his offspring in a fire despite his great efforts to save them at the risk of his own life. This is not to say, however, that all the characters herein are without nobility. When a Harvey Bailey risks death at the hands of his own desperate gang rather than take another man's life, or when Roger's friend weathers the gunfire of the guards on the wall rather than abandon his wounded partner, the reader is treated to the best of the human spirit. What then happens to the individual who has—at least in this moment—risen to the heroic image allows him, and in turn the reader, to experience real tragedy, or comedy, depending on the outcome. The fact that such displays of courage and virtue are possible for those who have not always performed admirably makes a further demand on the need for the synthesis of tragedy and comedy, with the implied recognition that few of us can reveal ourselves as pure saints or pure sinners, regardless of our stations or success in life. It is a matter, perhaps, of degree wherein the milieu of physical imprisonment prompts a clearer picture of the depths or heights to which men fall or rise. The fact that the same man can do both makes the problem of identities somewhat difficult to cope with, particularly as we are wont to classify people as either virtuous or debased. It is easier to accomplish this distortion when considering the man on the street, whose virtues or vices are more subtly demonstrated, than when drawing an image of the imprisoned man, who may display attributes of goodness on one occasion and on another occasion, the worst of human degradation. At times we feel disposed to toss off this dichotomy with facetiousness by saying "such are the ways of mice and men," but Mr. Johnson demands of us a more sober consideration of a world without comedians and without tragedians, where the tragicomedy emerges as a comic pathos of men searching for the selves they have not known in a world where they are forever strangers.

The Devil's Front Porch is an indictment; but this indictment is not so narrow that it calls to task those who are also caught up in the system they have been unable to change. Rather, the indictment is thrust against the immaturity of the human race, a decrying of the lethargy of the human soul in evolving the humanness of which, hopefully, it is capable.

This longing for the growth of kindness and understanding wraps the story in a sadness that gives a poignancy to even the lighter moments, and somewhere before the final page the reader is directed to explore his own relationships with his fellowman. The morality of the book thus emerges, and the relating of violence and sordidness and madness is vindicated in the final act of self-examination.

BILL D. SCHUL

Preface

I BEGAN writing this book with a strong determination to be accurate, terse, and, to the best of my ability, objective. I have endeavored to avoid permitting personal feelings to overshadow the facts. If I have failed in this respect, it is due to my inexperience and not to intent. To embellish in any way with false or exaggerated verbiage would defeat the real purpose of the book.

I believe this book to be different from most others written on the subject of prisons, as it is not a gathering of data from records which are sometimes faulty and incomplete, or from newspapers which usually report only what the officials and the prisoners wish to tell them. The incidents related herein are from actual experience of participating or from close association with the characters involved. The historical data comes from the files of the Kansas Historical Society and from the knowledge of men who served here at the time as either personnel or prisoners. The book was written within the confines of this prison and is the first one ever authorized and endorsed by its officials.

While this is primarily about the Kansas State Penitentiary, it should be understood that basically prisons are the same. Therefore, most of the happenings related could well be applied to any prison in our land. The characters mentioned herein were all men of national renown, criminally speaking. In some cases the names have been changed for various reasons, but for the most part, the real names are used.

The only thing I can promise the reader is that when the book is read carefully, he may put it down with a feeling of security and well-being, realizing how fortunate he is not to be one of the unfortunates mentioned in this book, and that he has been given a true and generous slice of prison life as it once was and as it is today.

I hope this book will show that although much progress has been made in our prison system over the years, there still remains much to be done before meaningful rehabilitation of prisoners can be realized. To the people who are interested in penal affairs this should inspire a challenge to utilize all of the psychological, technological, and educational tools available to them in this age of great advances.

The opinions and philosophies contained herein are my own and should be considered nothing more. They are based on nearly fifty years of experience and close association with crime, criminals, prisons, and prisoners, including more than forty years of imprisonment. The only doctorate I possess is from the "University of Experience."

I have omitted details in some cases, due to their repulsive nature. Otherwise I have not added to or detracted from the truth as nearly as it can be determined. When I found it necessary to mention what was generally conceded to be unfair or uncalled-for actions on the part of the officials or prisoners, I also tried to give a plausible and probable explanation as to the cause or causes.

I have refrained from using the true names of anyone still living unless I have permission to do so. This is especially true of anyone who is still in prison. I have no desire to embarrass anyone in any way.

It is my hope that this book will help to make the prisoner of today realize that he is fortunate in comparison with the men who served time many years ago. It may help them realize that someone is interested in their welfare and that they need only to take advantage of the opportunities available in order to find their way back to respectability—and, I hope, happiness. And lastly, I sincerely hope that each man who does find his way back will never reach such an altitude that he can't reach down and help another who lies in the same gutter in which he once lay.

My sincere thanks go to Mr. Charles D. McAtee, Director of Kansas Penal Institutions, and to Mr. Sherman H. Crouse, Warden of Kansas State Penitentiary, for granting me permission to write this book; to Mr. William E. Bain, Assistant Director of Probation and Parole, for his interest and confidence in my ability; and to all personnel and inmates who have encouraged me in this endeavor.

The *Kansas Historical Quarterly,* Leavenworth *Times* (1864–1916), Kansas City *Star* and *Times,* Topeka *Daily Capital,* and the many unmarked publications from which material was taken—my sincere thanks to these publications and to the many persons, living and dead, who contributed so much to this book.

LESTER DOUGLAS JOHNSON

The Devil's Front Porch

1

Early Days
at the Kansas State
Penitentiary

This too I know—and wise it were
If each could know the same—
That every prison that men build
Is built with bricks of shame,... *

IT WOULD be rather ludicrous to say that the Kansas State
Penitentiary was a bad prison. All prisons are bad. Suffice it
to say that from the time of its beginning, in 1864, up until
the late 1920's it was one of the most feared and hated prisons
in the United States.

The high, turreted walls with gun towers sprouting at each
corner, and the heavily armed, serious-looking guards who
patrolled them, accentuated the quiet and lack of physical
activity outside the vast structure. There was little to indicate
the cruelties and tortures which were taking place inside; one
could only guess, judging from what he had been told by men
who had been through the ordeal and were fortunate to have
lived to tell the story.

* All chapter epigraphs are excerpts from *The Ballad of Reading Gaol* by
Oscar Wilde.

Looking east from Military Road, across the rolling hills toward the muddy, swirling waters of the mighty Missouri River, this huge mass of stone and steel towered high above the heavy, settling mists of winter and the churning, shimmering heat waves of summer. By using the imagination, the casual observer could easily associate this feudal fortress scene with the days of King Arthur, expecting at any moment to see knights in shining armor, or a parade of ghostly specters appear out of the long-forgotten past.

There was little visible evidence to warn the unsuspecting wretch who was about to enter the big steel gates of the prison of the misery and despair, the cruelties and destruction to mind and body which would soon become stark reality to him inside this silo—the silo that accepted only human fodder to be decayed and fermented to the point of complete disregard for self-respect and pride, to utter insanity and ignominious death. Except for the grim eeriness of the high, unfriendly looking walls, there was no hint that within these portals of cold steel the hideous and painful fires of hate blazed fiercely. This was where many of the nation's most notorious criminals served their apprenticeships and where many ended their usually brief but bloody careers on the gallows or under blazing guns.

Foremost among the infamous characters who served time at Lansing was Emmett Dalton, the only survivor of the feared outlaw gang that dared attempt a doubleheader bank robbery at Coffeyville, Kansas, one October day in 1892. The citizens of the little town had been forewarned, and in the short but fierce gunbattle which followed, the rest of the gang, including Emmett's two brothers, Bob and Grat, were killed. Emmett was seriously wounded in the fight, was captured and sentenced to life imprisonment. After serving fifteen years, he was paroled in 1907 by Governor Hoch. It was reported that he married a childhood sweetheart and moved to California, where he became a successful businessman and a respected member of his community and his church. He apparently lived happily and profitably until his death not too many years ago. He was one of those rare characters who, after gaining recognition in the field of crime, never looked back when given another chance. He fought social prejudice and hatred with the only weapons available to an ex-convict at that time—self-confidence and determination.

Another early-day badman who served at Lansing was a maniacal killer called Lobo Cravens. He was a man of little talent except in the art of murder. He had been known to kill a man for nothing more than tossing a harmless joke his way. He was finally sentenced to Lansing, served a short time, and escaped. He was later apprehended, but not before he had killed several more men. He wound up his career in the Missouri State Penitentiary at Jefferson City.

Also among the early day inhabitants was "Coyote" Smith, a man who was noted both for upholding law and order and for wanton, indiscriminate killings, especially of Indians. He had a burning hate of the redskins and said all of them should be shot on sight. After a hectic and rather colorful career, he finally died, according to our information, in bed in St. Joseph, Missouri, his hometown.

In 1885 Willie Sells, a sixteen-year-old boy accused of murdering his family, began a life sentence and served twenty-one years before he was proven innocent and pardoned. His story is told in detail later in this book as he told it to the author.

The Roaring Twenties produced many well-publicized criminals, and Lansing received its share of them. Some were vicious, unscrupulous men, and all were dangerous. The most noteworthy of these were Alvin (Old Creepy) Karpis; Freddie Barker, one of the infamous "Ma" Barker's versatile sons, who was later killed with his mother by the FBI; Wilbur Underhill, known as "the Tri-State Terror"; and the inimitable Bill LaTrasse, the most likable and colorful man who ever held up a train single-handedly.

On the frontier at the close of the Civil War the only law with much authority was the law of the Colt, and it was administered freely, without mercy or regret. Men were killed for no other reason than the fear that they were about to kill someone else. Most of those who were sent to prison were potential candidates for some boot hill; and for that reason, if nothing else, it is not so strange that brutality, torture, and unrequited hard labor were meted out so promiscuously. There were no other methods known at that time for dealing with men who had grown up by the law of the gun and with the philosophy "Do unto others as you think they might do unto you."

There were no psychiatrists, psychologists, or penologists to teach the theory of rehabilitation—it is likely that if the word had been mentioned, most folks would have thought it was some new form of execution.

The system for handling convicted felons was more or less traditional. The idea seemed to be "Break him, or kill him," and that is exactly what they tried to do. This in spite of the fact that hundreds of years of trial and error had proven that this system was not effective in deterring crime. It failed to improve the attitudes of men and served only to carve more bitterness on what were already sorely wounded hearts. But the method was continued and expanded until it became almost unbelievable how some men could treat other humans.

The personnel in those days were not chosen for ability or outstanding intelligence. All a man needed to have going for him was a willingness to work long, dangerous hours for small pay, and the stomach for carrying out the prescribed brutalities. He was judged mostly on his ability to get a lot of work done with a minimum of trouble. If it was found that a guard abhorred blood and suffering, he was considered a weakling and didn't last long on the job. The guards wasted no time in letting the convict know that his only hope was to perhaps save his soul, but that the rest of his anatomy belonged to the state. The attitude of the officials during this era was best expressed by a sign which hung above the door inside the front gate. It read: "WHEN YOU ENTER HERE, LEAVE ALL HOPE BEHIND."

According to Mr. C. M. Lindsey, a former captain and deputy warden as early as 1908, and Willie Sells, one of the most controversial convicts to ever serve time here (1885–1907), it was not an uncommon sight to see a guard spit in a convict's face and dare him to wipe it off before it dried.

It made no difference, according to Mr. Lindsey, how long a man may have been held in some filthy, vermin-ridden jail, or how many dusty, sweaty miles he may have ridden or walked to get to Lansing, he was dressed-in without a bath or a chance to wash his face and hands. No attempt was made to see if he was vermin-laden. It made no difference. If he was, nothing was changed. If he wasn't, he soon would be.

Willie Sells, in describing his many years at Lansing, said, "The dirty, musty, tomblike cells were inhabited by various insects as well as rodents. Almost any prisoner could show red, angry-looking welts on his body from being bitten and stung by these pests over and over again. Most of the abrasions were infected and because of the lack of proper treatment, had become large, running sores. Little, if any effort was made to exterminate these invaders. The only variety of bug that experienced rough sledding was the head louse. There was good reason for this—no hair."

Those men of earlier years following the Civil War who were unfortunate and found themselves in this sinkhole of filth and perversion were men who had been ensnared in the unbreakable web of rebellion and nourished on its by-products—hate, prejudice, robbery, and murder. Little could they have realized that they played an important role in prison history which would lead to the renovation of a traditional, barbaric system and bring about its reform to some degree. They had no idea that they were the ones designated to blaze the brutal, punishing trail for posterity—to wear the badge of shame and be the guinea pigs for the uncertainties and mistakes that usually follow any experiment with human lives. They were the stepping stones to the more humane and scientific system which we of a later generation could at least tolerate.

While it is difficult to laud the officials of those trying times, it must be admitted that most of them did what they believed to be right, or the best they could under the existing circumstances. These men were untrained in prison administration and were mainly concerned with maintaining security and seeing that the sentences of the courts were carried out. They were frontiersmen first and prison officials last, and at no time were they humanitarians. They had many problems to solve and little more than brute force with which to do the job. They saw to it that the prison produced dollars, but did little to make it produce changed men.

The law did not instruct these men how to operate the prison. They did it as they thought they should, whichever way was the easiest and most effective. It is doubtful if any warden advocated the cruel methods used by many of the guards. They were probably tolerated simply because he was able to suggest nothing better. In many cases he was not aware of what was happening, or if he was, hesitated to rebuke the guilty parties because it was difficult to find men who would work in a prison for the small pay involved.

During this hectic period, from 1865 to the early 1900's, even as now, the warden had to be able to depend on his subordinates, and in many cases these assistants were not as dependable as they were believed to be. Most wardens were intelligent, methodical men, but were more interested in the political aspects of the position than in rehabilitative or reform measures aimed at teaching men how to live better lives.

Living conditions remained deplorable until the early 1920's because no one seemed to think that convicts deserved anything better, and there were no available funds with which to make improvements if it had been thought worthwhile to do so. The public was apparently satisfied with the system, and therefore no change was needed.

A new arrival's reception at the front gate was traditional. The procedure was born with the prison and was followed strictly until the late 1920's. In fact, except for the profanity, the clubs, and the tomfoolery, it is carried on in much the same manner today. The prisoner was turned over to a "dress-in" guard, a man who was picked for the job for his ability to harass and dish out sarcasm, and his eagerness to use the club he always carried. This specialist wasted no time in making the new man's future status clear. The instructions were brief but very definite and well punctuated by threatening gestures with the ever-present club, without which a guard would feel undressed. The old-time convict can remember the cutting words and the effect they always had on inexperienced men.

"Now, I want you bastards to listen good. If you remember what I tell you, it's possible that you will live to get out to rob, rape, steal, or kill again. This is a penitentiary, not a picnic ground. You will speak to no one except a guard, and that only when spoken to or given permission. When marching across the yard, you will look neither right nor left. You will keep your eyes looking straight ahead unless otherwise instructed. Now, line up in a column of twos and march when I give the word. We will get you fitted out in what the well-dressed convict wears at Lansing." It isn't likely that anyone who ever heard the silly, cackling laugh that always followed this sickly joke will ever forget. It was without any semblance of mirth and was certainly not encouraging.

After that came the booking, which consisted of one's telling his life history, like: how many times did your grandfather have the whooping cough, did your father beat your mother?—all that pertinent information regarding the fact that the prisoner stole a hog or perhaps some poor old lady's washtub. This stereotyped recitation seldom did much toward pepping up the prisoner, but it seemed to bolster the speaker's ego.

The next stop was the tailor shop. This was an experience never to be forgotten. It was a three-ring circus, complete with clowns—the prisoners. A long table sat in the center of a large room. About every three feet a convict stood behind a pile of merchandise. The first man issued shirts; the second, pants; the third, shoes; and so on down the line to the last man, who handed out miscellaneous articles such as suspenders, "bull's wool" socks, red bandannas, and various mine clothes.

The first man asked, "What size, Mac?" If the answer was "Fifteen," he threw him a nineteen, with the remark "Only got two sizes—too big and too little." If the customer told the pants man he wanted size thirty-two, he got at least size forty, along with a wisecrack, "You can make a spare pair out of what's left over." The shoe man was more obliging. He described his wares beforehand. "These come in five sizes: too big, too little, too stiff, too squeaky, and too damn heavy." Then he usually threw out a pair that would have fit Paul Bunyan. There was no exchanging articles after they had been issued. Almost always the buttonholes were too small for the buttons and far out of line. One shirt sleeve was always an inch or two longer than the other and twisted at a forty-five-degree angle. One fellow who served at Lansing at that time told me that when he called this to the attention of the guard, he replied, "So what? You ain't going anywhere in particular."

According to this informant, the pants were really a sensation. He said, "If you never wore a pair of pants made by a cow wrestler or a sod buster, then you ain't had a real experience." It was amazing how these monstrosities could keep a man stumbling and sideslipping. And this in the days when it was dangerous to stumble. The warning was "Don't stumble. If you do, you'll lose sight on the world." Some men were nearly decapitated for stumbling in the wrong direction at the wrong time.

Upon arrival at the receiving cellhouse, the first thing that caught the eye was a sign hanging at the corner of the second tier. It said, "QUIET." And that is exactly what it meant. Anyone who got the idea that this sign was just an ornament was in for a big surprise. No doubt there are some men still living who made that mistake and have some fine, well-developed knots on their heads to show for it.

In describing the punishments practiced in the early part of this century, reference must be made to them as "added" punishments. Just being in the prison was punishment enough to last the average man a lifetime. If he was one of those fortunate enough to escape the physical tortures, he was soon destroyed by mental anguish and monotony. The uncertainty of being permitted to live from day to day was nerve-racking enough to reduce what had once been strong, virile men to shambling wrecks without the will or desire to think for themselves or to act without directions. They could only hope for mercy, a thought that had to be secretly contemplated. Mercy was a word that was considered almost obscene. Many men went insane fearing that they might be subjected to the dreaded "water cure," or the crippling "cribs." These were two of the most painful and cruel punishments ever conceived in the mind of man. While some men did not survive these ordeals, many did, and it is from them that this information was obtained. Many of the men who served as guards at that time, as well as those who experienced the punishment, became emotional and sometimes nauseated while telling of the procedures.

I have been unable to locate any records to substantiate my belief that the water cure was invented at Lansing, nor do

I have anything to prove otherwise. However, it is safe to say that Lansing prison made it nationally known.

In the era around 1910 when the women of Kansas began to insist that brutality and torture must be abolished in our penitentiary, a painting of a man being subjected to this cruel punishment was hanging in the window of a restaurant in Topeka. This picture had been painted by an ex-convict who had been crippled for life by this inhuman device. It had plenty of viewers, and it served to further incense the decent people of Kansas, especially the ladies (bless them), who would accept no compromise—torture and crippling punishments had to go.

The water cure consisted of two separate phases. However, they were seldom, if ever, administered in quick succession to the same man. It is not likely that any man could have survived this. Just one was usually enough to make a man wish he hadn't "done it," or at least that he hadn't been caught "doing it."

The first and most diabolical phase of this punishment consisted of hanging a man by his thumbs with two small silver chains. He was then drawn up until his toes barely reached the floor. A four-inch fire hose was attached to a pressure pump. This hose had a nozzle with an outlet about the size of a dime. The water coming through such a small opening under such pressure was similar to a stiletto being plunged into the flesh. When it hit the face, the flesh was bruised and torn. If it hit the eyes directly, the eyes were gone. It had sufficient force to, and often did, knock out teeth, tear off noses, and shear off ears. When it was played directly on the midsection, it often mangled the intestines, causing severe, sometimes fatal, hemorrhages.

This treatment lasted as long as the guard who administered it, and who had originally recommended it, cared to continue. There was no court, no hearing, to determine whether or not the prisoner was guilty of a violation. If there had been, it would have made little difference. The prisoner would not have dared to insinuate that the guard lied. In order to receive this punishment, a convict did not need to say a word. If the guard said that he looked like he didn't like an order, that was enough.

The second phase of the water cure was not so painful physically as was the first, but it was equally, if not more, destructive. It took a terrible toll on the nervous system. The victim knew that if his stamina and physical ability was not at its best, he was likely to die at any moment. Several men did die from overexertion and fear of what could happen. This punishment, too, was administered at the whim of any guard who felt that he had been insulted or disobeyed, or who had a personal grudge against the victim. The one thing it was never applied for was missing task,* unless a man openly refused to try, for which there were other punishments.

In this case, the offender was placed in a steel tank about seven-feet deep. In the center of this tank was an adjustable hand pump. The victim was chained to this pump in such a position that he could neither rise nor kneel. The pump was adjusted to start picking up water when it reached the chin of the chained man—not before that time. The water was then turned into the tank, and the wretch could only watch it and try to prepare himself physically and mentally to try and pump it out faster than it came in, after the pump became active. If a man collapsed from fright, and some did, unless he had a guard who balked at murder, he was a gone gosling. Fortunately, there were a few who did draw the line at killing. It was not because of any sympathy for the convict; it was their own peace of mind that concerned them most.

I recall that when this was related to me, I said, "But surely, they wouldn't let a man drown." I couldn't believe that even in those hectic days such a thing could happen. However, I

* Work assignment or quota.

must have been wrong, because Mr. Lindsey told me of a case where death did occur and became just another incident, because there was practically no investigation into the death of a prisoner in those days—they all died of "natural causes."

The following incident was related to me by Mr. Lindsey and corroborated by Willie Sells and others who were in Lansing at the time. The victim in this case was a sixteen-year-old boy who was serving a sentence for larceny. He was a healthy, good-looking lad, and was apparently doing his best to cope with a bad situation. He was congenial and very careful to try and abide by the rules. The guard who was involved was supposedly a man of high integrity and character who possessed a better education than most of his fellow workers. It was later found, however, that he was also possessed of sadistic and homosexual tendencies which he had cleverly concealed behind the feigned mask of normalcy.

The guard had become enamored of this lad and had made every conceivable effort to get him to engage in perversion. The boy steadfastly refused, and in spite of all the promises and enticements the guard could offer, he would not submit. Finally, in maniacal desperation, the guard arranged to take the boy to the tank in an effort to break him down. He apparently chose the tank because he did not want to take the chance of disfiguring the boy's handsome face by subjecting him to the pressure hose. To mark or injure the boy severely would have made him unfit for the plans laid out for him.

During a cursory investigation which followed, the guard said that he had tried to turn the water off, but the valve stuck. Another guard, who had been present, at first backed this story. However, he later repudiated it and said that no attempt had been made to stop the water flow. It was then that it was learned that this guard had long been associated with homosexual practices, both inside the prison and outside. The final report was, as usual, "Death due to natural causes"; and the case was closed. I was acquainted with this guard many years later and have every reason to believe that he was a pervert of the worst type.

It is not likely that such a thing as this could happen today, because everyone is accountable to someone else in almost every situation. It would be nearly impossible to hide the facts for very long. It should also be admitted that there is a much superior breed of men in the penal system than there was at that time. It would be risky to say that there are not many incidents that need more explaining in every prison. There are; but none, I believe, as serious as the one just mentioned. We cannot tell the intents or the desires in the hearts of all men who work as prison guards, but we do know their limits and opportunities. And this, if nothing else, is insurance against any latent sadistic tendencies which might exist.

Although the water cure was a diabolical method of punishment, many thought that it was mild in comparison with the crippling "cribs." This latter device was responsible for a large number of convicts being deformed for life, both physically and mentally. It was said that if all other punishments were conceived by sons of satan, the cribs had to be the work of the Old Man himself—and he could well be proud of his work. Only a master craftsman with a horribly twisted mind could have produced such an inhuman contraption with which to crucify the body and soul of man.

This instrument was built in the shape of a coffin, and sat on rockers similar to those of an old-fashioned cradle. It was about two-feet wide, eighteen inches in depth, and varied in length. The lid, which screwed down tight, had a few small holes bored near the head to permit some ventilation. The inside was rough, with cross pieces every eight or nine inches for the purpose of adding to the discomfort.

The victim was stripped of all clothing. He was then shackled and his hands cuffed behind his back, after which he was placed face down in the box. The feet were pulled up to meet the hands and fastened in this position. The lid was then screwed down and the victim was left in this position for hours, according to the whim of the punishing guard. At intervals the convict was removed from the device and permitted to lie on the concrete floor for a little "rest." However, he was not unshackled or uncuffed, and was soon returned for another session in the box. This continued sometimes for weeks, or until the prisoner went stark, raving mad. Many of the weaker ones died within a few days from exertion and perhaps fear.

Many years ago I had an opportunity to see and talk with a few of the men who had survived these punishments. Some of them were deformed and hopelessly crippled from being subjected to these hellish devices. It is difficult for one to feel the full impact from just reading or hearing about these things, but when one can see the horrible results, it is something that will never escape the memory. It is gratifying to know that such things are not in use today.

I also managed to talk with one or two of the men who were known to have administered these punishments rather freely. I was amazed at the shallowness of their philosophies. They spoke of it as if it had been nothing more than a slap on the wrist, and in one case I am positive that I saw genuine pride in the eyes of the speaker. He said, "After all, they were just convicted felons. I had been appointed to punish them, and I did my job. No, I have no regrets."

Another painful and unusual punishment used during this same period was known as the hoist. It was not in the same class with the ones just mentioned, however it did produce some permanent injuries in a few cases. This method was used mostly on recalcitrant convicts, those who had the mistaken idea that they did not have to obey orders. Usually, one shot of this medicine changed their minds, and attitudes, with a minimum of delay.

As usual, the victim was stripped. He was taken to a special cell which had a large steel ring imbedded in the ceiling. The hands were cuffed behind the back, and one end of a long leather strap was snapped into the cuffs. The other end of the strap was passed through the ring in the ceiling, and the convict was drawn up until his toes barely reached the floor. He was left in this position until he passed out—which was not very long in most instances. He was then taken down, revived with water, and hoisted again—unless he was willing "to give it up, or tell where it was." The guards called it "listening to reason."

There were many other forms of punishment, but the ones just described were by far the worst. It was not uncommon for a convict to be beaten senseless in the presence of other convicts. It was thought that this would be good psychology, that it would instill fear in the hearts of those who witnessed the affair. These beatings took place mostly in the "contract" shops, where the state was responsible to outside interests for a certain amount of work, and the convicts were accountable to the state. This was during the period between 1900 and 1911.

The shop at Lansing was a shirt factory, and the state agreed to produce a given number of shirts each month at a price much cheaper than the cost would have been otherwise. Each man working in this shop was required to produce a "task"; that is to say, he had a number of shirts to produce or pay the consequences. Some men worked on sleeves, others on collars, and so forth. However, for every item over his required task the convict was given a few pennies in his account. This helped to buy tobacco and other items not furnished by the state.

The work was hard in this shop, and every workday was a twelve-hour one. Many found that at times they just could not continue. When this happened, they would stick their fingers under a needle or into some other part of the mechanism. This earned the victim a few days lay-in.* Finally, it became so obvious that it was a ruse that this excuse was outlawed. It was then called self-mutilation and resulted in the man being given first aid and returned to his bench. If he failed to get the task after this, he was subjected to a public beating and shoved off to the hole.

Up until 1910 when a man escaped, or attempted to do so, he was taken to the "bullring" and given a good working-over. When, and if, he recuperated, he was put on a long diet of bread and water. When he was released from the hole, a heavy ball and chain was attached to his ankle and was worn night and day, sometimes for several years. These men wore special-made trousers, so that one leg buttoned up the side in order that they could get their pants off without removing the shackle. In addition to this, a large red *E* was painted on his back and he was kept under close surveillance at all times. Besides these little inconveniences, the man lost all good time he might have earned—and at that time they could take all he would ever earn.

The bullring was a place, not a device; and what a place. It was situated beneath the tower at the southeast corner of the wall. This punishment was reserved for minor infractions, or to soften the man for a more serious punishment to follow. A man could be taken to this place for nothing more than accidentally kicking his waste bucket and making a little noise, talking in line, or getting out of lock step. The offender was usually taken from his cell early in the morning, before the other convicts were awake, and escorted to the tower by four or five guards. These guards were under orders to "leave him there, if you can." They usually could—and did.

When convicts were caught practicing homosexuality, they were fitted out in dresses and forced to wear them at all times. They also had a large red *P* stamped on their shirts or jackets,

---

* Permission to stay in from work.

designating them as punks, regardless of the nature of the act. Both the aggressor and the passive one were considered the same. Punk was the most shameful name given a man in prison, unless it was stoolie. Beyond this practice, there was little effort made to control this perversion. In fact, many of the officials thought it was amusing.

There was little freedom on the yard. The convicts were marched in lock step, and silence was demanded at all times. When a bell sounded in the cellhouse for a meal line to form, each man stepped from his cell and faced the front of the cellhouse. At a command, the line moved forward—all but the lead man, who waited. When all were within arm's length of each other, they simultaneously placed their left hands on the shoulder of the man in front of them. Another command, and all began to mark time, raising the right leg high and stomping it down hard. They moved in this fashion, and the cadence was kept until the line reached its destination. The right arm was swung in rhythm, and this presented a rather smooth, precisionlike march to the observer, but was very nerve-wracking to the convict. The least mistake on the part of the marcher assured him a trip to the bullring.

Willie Sells, who worked in the hospital, told me that some men were left lying in the bullring for hours before being brought to the hospital, and most of them looked as if they might have been hit by a passenger train. Others told me that they had seen guards leave this place with the heels kicked off their shoes, and their hands swollen from beating the convict. Mr. Lindsey, who was deputy warden at the time, told me of one guard who became so absorbed in his work that he ruptured himself and was forced to retire.

When a meal line filed into the dining room, the front tables were filled first. When leaving, those at the rear tables arose first. This way each man found himself in the exact place in line where he had been when he entered the hall.

This prevented any man from passing another at any time after leaving the cellhouse until he returned.

As each man took his seat, he folded his arms across his chest and sat erect until the signal was given to begin eating. When it was necessary to have something passed, no word was spoken. If he wanted salt and pepper, he made a sprinkling motion with his hands. If he wanted a slice of bread, he held up three fingers, and one of the passers would hand it to him on a long fork. If he desired an item that was in a pan, or the syrup pitcher, he made a circular sign with both hands. If he wanted pie—well, who didn't? The allotted time for eating was twenty minutes. At the end of that time a bell was sounded, and if a man hadn't eaten his food by that time— shame on him. All he could do was sit up straight, fold his arms, and stare at the food he wished he had eaten. And if there was a fairly large portion uneaten on his plate, the guard would write the convict's name and number on a piece of paper and send the plate and note back to the main steward; and no matter what it might be, he would be forced to eat it at the next meal before he could have anything else. When it came time to file out, as each man stepped into the aisle he immediately fell into lock step.

Upon reaching the cellhouse, each man stopped in front of his cell, stood at attention facing the door, and when the command was given, stepped quickly inside. He then turned again to face the door, put one hand on the bars, and remained in that position until the guard passed making the count. If anything other than a handkerchief had been found on a man during the frisk, he would be handcuffed to the cell door and left all night until time to go to the bullring next morning.

I recently read in an old newspaper clipping an article that said the prisoners at Lansing were being fed the very finest cuts of beef and pork. This was not true. According to Mr. Lindsey and others with whom I have discussed this matter, if those were the finest cuts, they must have been used before, as many guards had to leave the dining room because they could not stand the odor of the food. I was told of a rather amusing incident that happened in the mess hall one morning.

A young convict raised his hand and motioned to the guard that he wanted to talk to him. The guard walked over to the table. The convict held an object up for the guard to see and said, "Cap, I found a half a cockroach in my hash." The guard scratched his chin and meditated for a moment, then asked, "How long have you been here?"

The boy replied, "About a year."

"Uh-huh, that accounts for it," said the guard. "You haven't been here long enough yet to get a whole one. Better luck next time."

The old dining room was filthy and smelled like a hog pen at all times, but in summer it was almost unbearable. There were old softwood tables, and after a meal the remains were dumped on the table then scraped to one end with a wooden paddle. The swill gathered in the cracks, soured, and became putrid. This seemed to attract every fly in the surrounding area.

It is not surprising that an old timer shakes his head and smiles when he hears some young prisoner say, "Man, they got that old fried ham again for supper" or "That steak we had for supper last night was too tough and dry." Occasionally one says, "I wish they would change the dressing on the salad —I don't like French dressing" or "Why do they always have vanilla ice cream instead of mixing the flavors up?" One day I heard a fellow say, "We are having those braised beef tips too often, and the pork chops are not as lean as I like them." It is somewhat amusing to an old con who can remember when if they had served a pork chop, he would have been afraid to eat it.

It would be safe to say that the first slight improvement in prisons began about 1910 under Mr. J. K. Codding, who was warden at that time. Many of the sadistic and barbaric punishments were abolished then, not because of any noticeable change of heart on the part of the guards, but because of the pressure being brought to bear by the decent citizens who were fed up with such treatment. This does not necessarily mean that brutality ceased—it did not. If anything, the everyday routine treatment was as bad or worse. The guards carried the same-sized clubs and used them just as conscientiously, but perhaps a little more secretly. The convicts were still subject to personal grudges and were at the mercy of any guard who felt that he would like to punish someone. The bullring was still in the same place, and had just as much business as it ever did. (Incidentally, it is still there, although not in use.)

The lock step was abolished, and the silent system was enforced only in the dining room and in the cellhouses. Men could talk at work as long as they did their work and did not interfere with the other men. Smoking a pipe was allowed if tobacco could be obtained, but only in the cells and during the short periods on the yard in summer. To be caught smoking a cigarette, or having cigarette papers in their possession was almost high treason and was punishable by one year in the detention cellhouse—better known as Number Two.

This cellhouse has been more or less a mystery to the younger prisoners and officials. The building is one of the more interesting ones. It has been, in turn, the female prison, criminally insane ward, hospital, isolation and punishment, and death house. It has recently been abandoned, and at this writing, it is rumored that it may be converted into a chapel. If this is true, it will be rather interesting that a place of torture and fear will have become a place of worship.

This building was built in 1868 or 1869; it is difficult to be sure of which year. However, it is known that it was one of those two years, because there was, at one time, a date on the east side of the steps. The last number had been broken off, all but enough to tell that it had to be an *8* or *9*. On the other side of the steps was a red cross. What happened to the old steps, no one seems to know.

It was soon after 1910 that the little commissary which had been started by Jerry Choteau began to expand and the profits spent to buy baseball equipment for use when the prisoners were permitted to be on the yard. This store is still in operation, and the profits are consigned to the prisoners' fund. It is now a well-stocked store, and the men can buy almost anything within reason. It is because of this store that there is a movie each week and a fine football and baseball team—both outfitted from this fund. There are many other uses for this money of which very few people are aware. The trips taken outside by the choir (a very fine one) are financed from this fund, as are the many trips that the baseball team makes each summer.

The first change toward better living conditions began with the burning of the old north wing cellhouse. This was the oldest cellhouse and along with the south wing cellhouse formed the front wall of the prison. The building was destroyed by fire on the night of November 7, 1916. The Leavenworth *Times* of November 8, 1916, gave the following account of the conflagration:

WHILE 220 PRISONERS SLEEP IN LOCKED CELLS FIRE STARTS IN OIL-SOAKED ROOM

DESTROYS ROOF OF BUILDING

PRISONERS MARCHED TO SAFETY BY GUARDS—NO RIOTING—LEAVENWORTH FIRE DEPARTMENT MAKES RUN TO ASSIST

While 220 prisoners were locked in the north cell wing of the state prison at Lansing at 9:30 o'clock last night fire broke out in the fan room in the north end of the building and destroyed nearly the entire roof of the building before the prisoners, under the direction of officers were able to get it under control shortly after 11 o'clock. All the inmates were taken out safely.

A. C. Taylor was the only guard on duty in the cellhouse when the fire started and he was stationed at the south end and could not see the blaze. Cries of prisoners whose cells had filled with smoke notified him of the danger. Sounding the fire alarm he commenced unlocking the cells, each of which had to be opened individually. Guards of the day and night shift who had remained at the prison to get the election returns, rushed to the cellhouse and the prisoners were marched out and taken to the south wing cellhouse.

Perfect order was preserved by the convicts and they gave the guards no trouble. There was no danger of a riot at any time. After the men had all been removed from the cellhouse the guards selected a bunch of prisoners and put them to fighting the fire which had gone through the roof and was leaping toward the sky feeding on the tar paper roofing with which the roof was covered.

Both Warden J. K. Codding and Deputy Warden C. A. Tolman were out of town bringing in prisoners. Captain C. M. Lindsey and Captain J. W. Burns took charge and directed the work. [Mr. Lindsey later became deputy warden, and Mr. Burns became Bertillon man. Mr. Burns was later killed in the line of duty.]

While discussing this many years laters, Mr. Lindsey recalled something that the reporter did not know—or did not care to mention. The convicts were removed under heavy shotgun guard, because most of the most dangerous men were quartered in this cellhouse. He also stated that there were no visible signs of impending trouble. The newspaper article continued:

Guard Taylor put out lights in the men's cells at 9:00 o'clock and returned to his post. As soon as the convicts gave the alarm he notified the rest of the guards outside. The cellhouse is locked from the outside, so Taylor was a prisoner with his men even after the cells were opened. The guards outside immediately unlocked the house and there was no delay. Mr. Taylor declared the convicts kept perfect order.

PRISONERS SHOWED BRAVERY

The convict firefighters showed as much bravery as if they were not preserving their own prison. Dragging the heavy hose lines through suffocating clouds of smoke, they went clear to the roof and played the streams where they would do the most good. Not one faltered or hung back. In fact, the guards had more volunteers for service than they could use.

The only evidence of excitement shown by the prisoners was when the Leavenworth fire truck drove into the yard. Cheer after cheer greeted its warning signal.

This news article of fifty years ago has been included in these pages because it heralded the beginning of a new era in prison administration. The change has been slow, as it was expected to be, but this was the start which finally led to a more humane and effective prison system such as we have today. It brought about the first real effort to make living conditions more bearable.

When reconstruction of the destroyed north wing was finally decided upon, it began with a plan which in those days was considered foolhardy. It was to be completely rebuilt and made into a dormitory-like cellhouse. The cells would have no bars, and it would be exclusively for honor prisoners. It took five years to complete this job; but when it was ready for occupancy in 1921, it was a structure that Kansas could well be proud of—one that a few years earlier the skeptics had said would be a total failure.

This new cellhouse worked well from the start and has since been greatly improved upon. Where once the guards patrolled the catwalks, watching each cell and its occupants, there are now television sets situated at convenient spots where the men can watch their choice of three channels each

evening from three until twelve. Where once nothing but
silence was tolerated, there are radio earphones in each cell
and, here too, there is a choice of three stations. The radio is
controlled by a master set in the control center. These are on
twenty-four hours a day.

When at one time all a convict could do was sit and look
out of his cell at bare, dirty walls thick with cobwebs, he now
sees a wall painted sea-foam green. These walls are given a
new coat of paint each spring and are kept spotlessly clean at
all times. The cells, which were dirty and musty, dark and
odorous, are now painted a bright yellow and trimmed in
black. The beds are now equipped with springs and stand
two high. It is a far cry from the cellhouse of 1866.

In 1925 the first locked modern cellhouse in the prison was
erected on the spot where an old stone horse barn once stood
at the northwest corner of the yard. This was also the first
cellhouse to have six-man cells. These large cells are situated
in the two top tiers on each side. In 1927 the south and east
wings were remodeled and made modern. Instead of the cell
fronts being solid stone, two-feet thick, they are now barred,
giving more light and ventilation. The doors slide back and
forth instead of opening out. The locking system is automatic, permitting the opening of one door on a tier or all at
one time, as desired. Each of these cells is also equipped with
earphones.

Shortly after the honor dormitory was opened, it was decided to experiment with an intermediate dormitory. The
bars of the old south wing were ordered removed. The only
difference in it and the honor dormitory was that this one
would be supervised by a guard both day and night. The
honor dormitory was—and is—supervised by convicts under
the direction of a lieutenant. The idea was to institute a new
method of grading the new prisoners. When they first arrived
and for six months thereafter, they would be third-grade
prisoners. This would mean that they would be in a locked

cellhouse and kept under strict surveillance until more was known about their attitudes and their intentions. The purpose of this evaluation was to prevent troublemakers from instigating anything that was not expected. After six months, if the man had shown himself to be trustworthy and willing to adjust properly, he could apply for transfer to the intermediate dormitory and second class. From this point on he would have to earn his way to the honor dormitory and first class.

2

---•◆•---

Initiation
at the Devil's
Front Porch

And bound with bars, lest Christ should see
How men their brothers maim.

THINGS HAD changed very little as far as living conditions and treatment were concerned in the early 1920's. The guards, while of a slightly more civilized type, were still filled with hatred for a convict, and they still carried the big clubs with which to emphasize that hatred. This was undoubtedly due to the facts that most of them were illiterate and that tradition still ruled the system, as it does today in many cases.

There was a bit more freedom of the yard, and athletics were tolerated to a point. This, however, served to cause more bloodshed. There was a ring of hoodlums involving both guards and convicts who fixed every contest, and woe be unto the man who refused to cooperate or who doublecrossed. If the dreaded Cosa Nostra of today thinks it is a unique organization, it is badly mistaken, as will be shown later on in this book.

I first arrived at the Kansas State Penitentiary on March 12, 1924, along with seventeen other prisoners. We came in a special railroad car. We had been ordered transferred to

28

Lansing because we were suspected of starting the fire at the reformatory in Hutchinson, which almost completely destroyed the main buildings of that institution in January, 1923. As we unloaded at the little Santa Fe station we could see the grim, rough walls atop a high hill about a mile to the east. There was little activity to be seen outside those walls, but I was sure of the misery and degradation taking place inside this much-hated and -feared prison. I had read the books *The Twin Hells* and *The Kansas Inferno,* both written by men who had served at Lansing many years before. I thought I had learned enough from them to be able to cope with any situation which might arise. I was dead wrong. I only found out how little I knew and how little the authors knew—or were able to tell.

The first thing I found out was that there was no such thing as mercy or understanding here. The first guard I saw looked at me as if I had just scalped his entire family. He tucked his abbreviated baseball bat under one arm as if he was reluctant to turn loose of it. He pulled a piece of paper from his pocket, squinted at it, then spoke.

"All right, you mangy looking bunch of bastards. Cut out the talking and pay attention. You ain't in the reformatory now. This is a penitentiary, and you'll find out damn quick that you ain't tough. We tame leather-asses here, and you ain't no exception. Now, when I call your name, answer, and answer loud. This may be the last time you'll hear it—we don't name the cattle here."

I had always been under the impression that the numbering of prisoners was to facilitate the keeping of records—place of work, cell location, and so forth. Perhaps this was true in a sense. However, it may have gone deeper than that. When a man has his individuality taken from him, it seems to do something to his pride. He feels ashamed and degraded, and this is conducive to a severe inferiority complex. The officials must have realized this fact—if it is a fact—because they seemed to glory in reminding the prisoner that he had no name, just a number. One prisoner's referring to another as "mister" was grounds for at least a good bawling out, or perhaps a rap or two on the head with one of those lethal "saplings" that no guard was ever without. At one time there was an attempt made by some eager beaver to forbid anyone writing to a convict to address the letter "Mr." This idea met with so much opposition outside—some of it legal—that the idea was abandoned. However, even at this late date a prisoner may not sign his name in this manner. Most men learn to accept this and consider it part of their penalty, but this was not always the feeling.

It is almost impossible to describe the emotion that grips a man as he walks up the sidewalk toward the gates of a prison, knowing that in another few minutes he will be swallowed up inside a silo of stone and steel, where he will slowly but surely ferment and decay unless he happens to be one of the lucky or stronger ones. It is doubtful if any two men have feelings alike at such a moment. It may be a matter of temperament and latent character, and whether or not he has been able to reconcile himself to any extent. Some men realize that they do have a choice and that it must be made immediately and definitely. They can choose to try and make the best of a bad situation and spare themselves a lot of physical and mental pain, or they can choose to buck the expected slot set aside for them and by so doing, reduce their chances of survival. If a man is foolish enough to choose the latter course and is fortunate enough to survive, it is almost a certainty that he will be so bitter and filled with hatred that it might have been better for him to have died at the outset of his incarceration. He will be a dead mortal cinch to spend the rest of his life in some prison if he is not killed by some equally bitter inmate or by police during one of his short excursions outside between sentences.

I know that I felt as small and alone as I had ever felt in

my life, in spite of the fact that I had some foreknowledge of Lansing prison. In that brief moment I had lost any arrogance or bravado that I might have possessed before. I knew I was not going to buck the odds. I decided to play it by ear and see what happened.

When those steel gates clanged shut behind me and I found myself in the prison yard, I glanced at the prisoners passing by. One could not help but notice the thin, sickly pallor of their skin and the vacant, faraway look in their eyes. They seemed to shuffle rather than walk—somewhat like mechanical men. Each step seemed to drag as if their shoes were loaded with lead. They looked neither right nor left. They spoke not a word. In fact they seemed not to notice each other.

This was the human silage of which I had read so much. Men on the way to deterioration of mind and body. They were but shells of what must have once been healthy, robust men. Some were old men, some middle-aged, and some boys who would have been more at home in some grade school than in a penitentiary. Even the youngest ones were already showing the effects of the monotonous routine, the brutality, and the perversion. Some of them tried to smile, but it was a pitiful attempt without a trace of mirth—only a sickly grin, showing abject misery, lost hope, and perhaps homesickness. I know that at that very moment nostalgia was eating at my heart like a canker sore.

The guards were all dressed differently. Some wore big white hats, blue shirts, and cowboy boots, while others wore shirts and trousers with old-fashioned engineer's caps perched atop their heads. They all carried the large clubs with a leather thong around their wrists, ready for instant use. Among them I cannot recall ever seeing a genuine smile or any sign of compassion. I remember that I wondered what it could be that would so harden men's hearts toward other men who had done nothing to them personally. Finally, I concluded that it was not us they hated, but rather what we represented. To them we were symbols of everything that was evil. Tradition had taught them this, and I doubted that it would ever be completely forgotton—traditions die hard. To the guards we stood for hate, viciousness, and danger for all law-abiding citizens. As these thoughts ran through my mind I realized that the guards were also symbols to the convict: bitter enmity, persecution, and sadism. Neither side ever gave thought to trying to understand the other. It was dog eat dog —and the guards were the ones with the largest teeth.

The one thing that is deeply etched in my memory is the moment I first stepped into the receiving cellhouse. The only sound to be heard was the slap-slap of the slippers worn by the turnkey as he came forward to meet us. However, the most noticeable feature was the strange odor which seemed to permeate the entire building. It was one that I have tried to describe many times since and have failed. It was a musty odor that seemed to drift in and out with almost precise regularity. I had never smelled anything like it before, and except in that house I have never experienced it since. As the turnkey drew closer, I noticed that he, too, carried a club. It hung from his belt along with a large ring of keys. As he brushed by me, the first odor I had noticed was overshadowed by one of human filth. He was heavily bearded, and the beard was matted with tobacco juice which could easily be seen dripping from the corners of his mouth. His shirt was unbuttoned to the waist, and I could see that it was actually black around the collar and down the front. It was not difficult to imagine what it looked like in places which were concealed. I remembered that I had, on occasions, been close to men who worked on scavenger wagons, and they were much more pleasant to be around than was this guard. I must admit in all fairness that he was an exception to the general rule. Most of the guards did keep neat and clean, at least externally.

As I stood there thinking what a terrible-looking character this fellow was, I looked around at my companions and myself. As I did, I almost committed the unpardonable crime of laughing. There we stood, clutching the spare clothing and other paraphernalia they had issued us—extra pants and shirt, and little odds and ends—and at the same time trying desperately to hold up the pants we were wearing and to keep from walking out of the scows they called shoes. And besides that, we were a frightened group of young fellows. We tried to hide this fear, but it broke through like the headlight on a passenger train. Genuine fear can never be concealed.

There was a small barbershop on the opposite side of the cellblock, and that was our next stop. We lined up, and the first man got into the chair. He was a nice-looking young fellow with a wealth of curly blond hair of which he was very proud—and very touchy.

The convict-barber fingered the golden locks and asked, "Do you want to keep this hair?" The boy replied that he certainly did. The barber took three snips and handed the hair to its owner. "Here you are. I'll give you the rest of it in a minute." I won't say that boy was angry, but if looks could break bones, that barber would have been in a cast the rest of his life. He did get seriously injured a few months later by this same boy. However, I am not sure that it was because of this incident. When I got into the chair I said, "Take it all off. I never did like long hair anyhow." It had always been my motto, "If you can't beat 'em, join 'em."

A few minutes later I found myself locked in one of the dark, tomblike cells. I sat down on the dirty, vermin-ridden straw ticks and took a good look. I realized that this was the moment of truth—the beginning of a long, horrible nightmare that would end only with freedom, which seemed so far away, or death, which could possibly be very near. I was in the hands of men who cared less than a damn whether or not I lived another minute. I confess that a few tears fell as intense loneliness took command of my emotions. I wondered how long it would be before I began to look like those poor wretches I had seen as I crossed the yard. How long could I hold out against this miserable, filthy existence without going stark raving mad?

As I sat surveying the meager furnishings, I noticed that the vermin had wasted no time going to work. I spent the next ten minutes defending myself, then began an inventory. There was a rickety table, two small stools, a small water bucket hanging on the door, and a larger one sitting in a rear corner. The table had one very small picture sitting on it—a photo of a beautiful lady. It sat on a homemade scarf, and I could tell that it had been handled a lot. The bunk was merely several slats fastened together by steel straps at each end and in the center. It was more like a manger, at least a foot deep. It turned up at the outside edges, and in order to get into it, you had to crawl up and fall in. Coming out, you did this in reverse. The smelly, oily-looking straw tick was hard and lumpy, and there was one torn, filthy blanket. This was the size of the fixtures.

The front of the cells were of solid stone about two feet in width. The only opening was the door, which opened out and had to be locked with a key. At night there was a safety bar which dropped down over the door when a lever was manipulated at the end of the tier. I sat there and contemplated the possibilities, both good and bad, which certainly lay ahead. A large rat darted into the cell through a small aperture in the rear which was supposed to be a ventilator. In a few minutes I had seen mice, as well as almost every kind of insect known to man, scurry across the floor.

This was it. My first day in the Kansas State Penitentiary, "The Devil's Front Porch." It had been one of the most hectic days I could remember ever having lived, and yet it was rather tame in comparison with the many which followed.

That first night was like a trip to Dante's Inferno, and it would have been worse if I had not been fortunate enough to be put in a cell with a man whom I had once known. I felt comparatively safe with him, in spite of the fact that he had been convicted of brutal murder. His name was Rufus King. I had been only a small boy when I knew him, and it took some time for me to make him understand who I was. When he came in from work we began talking about old times, and I hoped he would say something about his case, but he avoided that. However, I knew most of the facts as they were brought out at his trial.

Rufus had once been a successful dirt contractor and was a Spanish-American War veteran. He had made some faulty calculations in a government bid and had lost about everything he had. He then came home to Maple Hill, Kansas, and opened a livery stable. He did well at this, although he was not getting rich. It was never proven that Rufus was in real bad financial difficulties, and I do not believe this was what prompted him to commit the crimes of which he was accused.

A young man named Woody, who lived at nearby Rossville, Kansas, and who was known to be a friend of Rufus's, came up missing. This was in 1918. There was little doubt that the boy had met with foul play. Rufus was questioned, but was hardly suspected. A prolonged and thorough search failed to produce the body of the missing youth, and it is likely that had another mysterious disappearance not occurred in the vicinity, the Woody case might never have been solved and Rufus King would not have been convicted. However, when the authorities received a query from some people back East regarding the whereabouts of two of their relatives who had last been heard from at Maple Hill, the investigation was reopened in earnest. The first one to suspect Rufus was a young newspaper reporter from Topeka. He obtained permission to investigate on his own, and he finally uncovered sufficient evidence to warrant the search of the premises where Rufus lived. The results of this search were astounding. The body of young Woody was found on the home premises, and the bodies of the wayfarers—a man and wife about sixty years of age—were found at the barn, buried in a manure pile beneath the carcass of a horse. Rufus was arrested and still maintained that he was innocent, in spite of the fact that he still had possession of the couple's wagon and horses. He said he had bought them, and the couple had left for California. Then came the clincher. Woody's watch—the one he had been wearing at the time of his disappearance—was found in Rufus's possession. The owner's name was engraved on it. Rufus also claimed that he had loaned Woody money on it.

Rufus was arrested and charged with the murder of young Woody. It was while he was in the Shawnee County jail at Topeka that he became the subject of much favorable gossip. It was at this time that an epidemic of the deadly Spanish influenza hit the nation, and people were dying like flies, even falling dead on the street. The prisoners in the Topeka jail were not immune—that is, none but Rufus King. He stayed up night and day, refusing to rest, and administered to the sick inmates. Miraculously, he was not ill one day, and the medical authorities said he did a wonderful job. Many of the prisoners owed their lives to this strange man. He refused to accept any reward, saying that he would do as much for a sick dog. He received much publicity, and regardless of what might be said, this had a bearing on the fact that it took nearly three years to convict him. Of course, it is true that he was a member in good standing with one of the strongest fraternal organizations on earth, and they did all they could to help.

Rufus appealed his conviction and while awaiting the decision of the high court, drove a transfer wagon in Topeka. I used to ride with him and happened to be aboard on the day the officers stopped his wagon and informed him that the Supreme Court had denied his appeal.

Time went by quickly as we talked about Topeka and Maple Hill, where I also had relatives. A bell sounded, and Rufus told me it was the signal to retire. We had five minutes to get undressed and get into bed. If we were caught out of bed or with our clothes on when the guard came by, we were subject to report for attempt to escape.

Rufus reminded me that if I should have to get up in the night for any reason, I should be sure to put my shoes on. Failure to do this could result in severe rat bites. He told me not to pay any attention to the odd sounds I might hear, as hardly a night passed that some fellow did not go berserk, to be carried away to the criminally insane ward to be chained, beaten, and to await death—merciful death.

I lay for a long time with my thoughts, and wondered when and where it would all end. I was confused and befuddled, and it didn't help my nerves any to hear a big rat trying to get the lid off the waste bucket. Without any light in the cell, I could see where some fellow before me had squashed bedbugs on the whitewashed walls, leaving red smears. The wall looked like a dirty tablecloth that had been hung up from corner to corner. It wasn't long before I was contributing to the ugly design. The bedbugs were having a ball; I concluded that they had been on rather short rations for some time and were trying to catch up. I captured a couple and found that they were not bedbugs, but body lice. The place was infested. They came in swarms and did their best to burrow into the flesh. When they had eaten their fill, they scampered up or down the wall looking for a place to sleep off the overload.

I found it impossible to sleep, so I lay and watched the insect hordes romp around the cell. They darted in and out of the thin shaft of light that shone through the bars of the door. The walls had been perspiring, and the water had run down, forming little rivulets. It was interesting to watch the bugs try to get from one side to the other; they sort of reminded me of my own predicament—utterly frustrated. They, like myself, were faced with a problem to which there seemed to be no sensible solution. Occasionally, one would get trapped in the tiny stream and fight furiously to get free. When he did succeed and scurried away, he left a faint trail of water. This was what I had to do—fight to get free and not give up until I had done so. But I also realized that I must fight with wits and not with brawn. In fact, I was always a bit short of brawn. On the other hand, I prided myself on the fact that I was usually a good thinker and not given to false pride. I could bow down with the best of them.

I do not know how long I had lain—I must have dozed. But I was awakened by a commotion somewhere further down the tier. I heard a shout, and in a couple of minutes, two figures rushed down the walk carrying a stretcher. In a few minutes they came back, and we could see that there was someone being carried. Rufus asked the guard what had happened. The guard, a big, clownish-looking man, stopped, put his hands on his hips, and said, "Oh, some damn fool hung himself." He stomped angrily and added, "They pick the damndest times to do these fool things. I was right in the middle of a rip-roaring western story."

I wondered what kind of people these were who held human life so cheaply. How could even illiterate and ignorant people be so heartless? It was apparent that this was but a sample of how most guards felt about their charges. Mercy and compassion were words that had no place in their vocabulary—certainly not in their hearts.

The rest of the night was filled with the thud of clubs as a man was beaten for some infraction—or perhaps in my fear I imagined that was what I was hearing. However, I was not dreaming when I heard the filthy language of the guards as they went about their work. Occasionally, I could hear the pitiful pleading of a young boy as he tried to escape the shame of submitting to a pervert, and the idiotic laughter of those who were indulging in a wild orgy of homosexuality.

No dawn was ever quite so welcome to me as the one which followed that night. I hoped that it would never get dark again and that somehow I could shut out the hideous sounds I had heard during the last few hours, which still rung in my ears. But there was little time for regret or to do any wishing. We had only about ten minutes to wash our hands by one holding his hands over the waste bucket while the other poured water sparingly from the little pail which seldom had more than a quart of water in it early in the morning. Then we had to grab the waste bucket and rush out to join the famous Bucket Brigade. This was the name given to the line which formed every morning, rain, sleet, and snow notwithstanding, and walked, sloshed, or slid through the weather to the coldest corner in the prison, where the cesspool was situated. This first morning was an experience that I could never forget, and I remember that I was thankful that it was not winter at the time.

The men came from the south wing and the east wing and had to stand in line and await their turn. This meant that sometimes we had to stand in line for fifteen or twenty minutes before getting to the cesspool.

I don't think the novelist Zane Grey ever visited this penitentiary, but if he did and it happened to be at the time the Bucket Brigade was in action, I would wager that it was then that he got his first idea for his great book *The Thundering Herd.* To see men sloshing through the snow and slipping and sliding on the ice, sprinkling everyone near with the contents of the buckets, was a spectacle worth seeing. But this was not the worst of the deal. It happened at breakfast time, and there was seldom time to get back to the cell and wash; and if there had been, it is not likely that there would have been any water with which to do the job. It was difficult to tell which was the most obnoxious, the cesspool or the dining room.

There had been some improvement in the serving of food and its quality since the days that Mr. Lindsey and Willie Sells had told me about. The standard menu now consisted of two slices of fresh side meat, rendered until it could be crushed with a fork, syrup, bread, and coffee. The favorite procedure was to crush the meat and mix it with syrup. Occasionally there was dry oatmeal, but no sugar or milk. This was also mixed with syrup. If we had gravy, which we did on occasions, it was the same procedure. I have often shuddered to think what would become of us if it had not been for that syrup. At noon we usually had some watery beans with no meat seasoning, or potatoes boiled in broth (water). But we still had the syrup to fall back on. At night there was usually some soup, bread, and coffee—and syrup. However, what we did have was palatable, and that was something.

There had been little change in the living conditions. We still had portal-to-portal bars, wall-to-wall concrete, and hot and cold running guards. We had a burlap towel in the cell, and it was possible to get a straw pillow, if you had the necessary funds and the right connections. We were issued one small bag of tobacco each week, and a corncob pipe. The tobacco was named Humming Bird; we called it Stool Pigeon.

After breakfast on that first morning we were taken to the office of the deputy warden. He was a nice-looking man and very brisk and businesslike, and not monkey-business-like either, as we soon discovered. I cannot tell all that went on at this meeting, because most of it would not be fit for anyone to read. If any man was in doubt as to what would be expected of him during his stay here, it vanished as the interview progressed.

The deputy seemed not to notice us at first. He fiddled with some papers on his desk. Suddenly he looked up and said, "I'm sorry. My porter must have forgotten to furnish chairs for you gentlemen to sit in. But, it's just as well," and now he roared, "because if I caught one of you sitting in a chair in this office, I'd knock hell out of you." He hesitated, his face turned red with anger, then he continued.

"I guess you realize that you have been sent here to serve a sentence at hard labor. Well, I intend to see that you do just that. I had nothing to do with you coming here, and I don't know whether you are guilty or innocent—probably innocent. Most of you are. It makes not a bit of difference to me if you ever get out. That is your own problem. Just do as you're told, and you may make it. There is no easy way here, but you can make it just a little less miserable by walking the line." He picked up a small book from the desk and waved it over his head.

"This," he said, "is your Bible from now on. Follow what it says and you will accumulate a lot less knots on your head." He put the book down and walked around the desk and faced us close-up, as if he was about to let us in on a secret.

"Now, every damn one of you are going to catch the 7:20 tomorrow morning. [That meant we were going to the mine. This term came from the fact that the shaft was 720 feet deep.] When you get there the officers in charge will assign you to a place of work—and I do mean work with a capital *W*. You will be given a task, which means you will have a certain amount of coal to produce for the state each week. The amount will be determined by the condition of the place where you will work. But whatever it is, I want it. I don't care how you get it—you can dig it, steal it, or get it with your good looks and charm—but get it." He motioned the guard to take us away.

We spent the rest of that day digging a ditch, looking for a water line that existed only in some eager-beaver guard's mind. After we had dug down six feet, another guard came along and told us to cover it back up—it was a mistake. By the time we had filled the hole up again, it was time for supper. We were given about ten minutes to clean up. We went to eat, then were taken back to the cellhouse to toss and tumble all night, listening to the eerie sounds, and to try and steel ourselves for the ordeal we knew was coming with the next dawn—the trip to the bowels of the earth, where for all we knew, we would be crippled or maybe killed without delay. That night was one of fear and apprehension, but I was so tired that I slept fairly well. When dawn finally did come, I could feel that heavy load tugging at my stomach, which I had now learned to identify with fear.

3

The Mine

The vilest deeds like poison weeds,
Bloom well in prison-air; . . .

AFTER THE usual morning assault on the cesspool and gagging
my way through breakfast, a guard escorted me through the
north gate to the mine top. I was furnished with additional
equipment, including a small can of carbide, which I learned
later was one thing in the mine that a man should not be
caught without at any time. One of the convicts showed me
what to do with it. He unscrewed the bottom off my lamp
and filled it almost half-full of little carbide chunks. He put
water in the top of the light, turned a little handle, and waited
a moment for it to generate. Then he placed one hand over
the reflector to trap the gas emerging from the flue, then suddenly pulled the hand away in a sliding motion which caused
the small wheel to scratch the flint, making a spark which
ignited the gas. Then he extinguished the light, and as he
handed it to me, he asked, "Did you see how it was done?" I
assured him that I had, but I was careful not to tell him that
I could do it. I really doubted that.

I watched, fascinated by the big cages speeding by—one up,
one down. Coal dust and dirt showered me as I stood waiting
while the loaded car was dumped into the hopper high above,
to be weighed and distributed to outgoing railroad cars, the

43

Nickle Plate, and the local bins. The Nickle Plate was the name of a small narrow-gauge track upon which convicts pushed coal to the power plant, which was at that time situated inside the main walls. The railroad transferred coal to the various state institutions, and the rest was for the use of employees.

At last the engineer stopped a down-bound cage right in front of where I stood. The guard said, "Get in the car, sit down, keep your hands off the sides of the car, and do not get up until you are told—and do not light your lamps." I thought he must be kidding. I wasn't about to stand up; I doubt if I could have. I knew as much about lighting that lamp as I did about mining coal, which was what someone had told me that I couldn't remember. But I crawled into a car with nine other souls in pain and flopped down like a sack of corn. We acted just as if we were not afraid, and I know I was wondering how hard we would hit the bottom. I had always remembered an old saying that my dad used. He said it wasn't the falling that hurt a person; it was the sudden stop. Without warning, the bottom seemed to drop out of the world, and all I could hear was the mournful whistling of the wind and the rattling and banging of chains.

Just as suddenly as we had been dropped, we began to slow up. There was a gentle bump, and I could see that we had arrived in the hated and feared coal mine—that is, all except my stomach, which arrived a few seconds late. Someone yelled, "Stay down, don't get up!" I looked and almost lost my breath when I saw a huge chunk of coal headed my way at a fast clip. It hit our car with a terrific bump, and we began moving backward. Then I knew that it was a car of coal with a large piece for an end board, which I had seen. I finished swallowing what was left of my heart and relaxed as the monsterlike car jumped off the bottom and headed for topside.

Two convicts pushed our car around the cage on a side rail to where a big evil-looking bearded guard stood with his hands on his hips. He squirted some tobacco juice about twenty feet and roared, "All right, get your asses out here and let me see what they sent this time." As we climbed out and stood on shaking legs, he looked us over critically, grinned one of the most idiotic grins I had ever seen, then reared back and said, "By god, the longer they come, the worse they get." The leer on his face would have told me that he was a guard even if I hadn't known it. I knew that no one in the world could leer like a guard. The expression on his face could only mean disgust at such a puny array of alleged coal miners. "Hell," he continued, "you bums couldn't dig enough coal in a month to cremate a mosquito. Where in the hell do they dig up characters like you who ain't big enough to hurt anyone. You don't look smart enough to be a thief. What are you—a rapo*?" He looked right at me as he spoke.

I thought this was a good place for me to try diplomacy, so I assured him I was not a rapo, but that he was probably right on the other counts. I figured if I copped out to being an idiot, he might have a little mercy on me. But it didn't work.

"Oho," he chortled. So that's it. A con man, eh? Well, let me tell you something or other, Rube, I been to two county fairs myself, and you ain't fooling me."

He then assigned me to a division that all men dreaded, Old Easy Seven. Because of the location of this division, the usually shifting weight of the mine sat still on this particular spot. At least, that is how it was explained to me. The coal miner had to depend on the shifting weight of the earth to aid him in several ways. First, it loosened the boulders and floor dirt. Second, when the room was dug about a pick-handle deep (this means that the fine dirt had been taken from beneath the coal to the depth of an ordinary pick handle) and left overnight with sprags beneath it, the earth, shifting properly, would break the coal off to that depth. This

---

* One convicted of rape.

made it necessary for the miner to merely knock out the sprags the next morning, and the coal would usually fall without trouble.

It is next to impossible to describe with any degree of accuracy what the coal mine looked like unless the reader has at least been down in one of some sort. It is wholly inadequate to say that it was a complex series of tunnels with twists and turns. And yet, that is exactly what it was. One has to imagine an underground city of complete darkness except for the meager bit of light that came from a carbide lamp worn on the miner's cap. There were crooked, winding roadways littered with rocks and dirt. The temperature stayed about the same both winter and summer. It was about forty-five degrees at the face in an air course, to seventy or eighty degrees in other parts of the mine. There was always an odor of musty, rotting wood and slate dust which was not at all unpleasant and could not be found in any other place except a coal mine. Of course, around the bottom and the mule barn this odor was superceded by those common to such an environment. About the only difference in this section and that of a country barnyard was there were no pigs grunting or hens cackling. The convicts did the grunting, and the guards did the cackling.

I suppose the most noticeable thing about a mine, when you were away from the main roadways or the diggings, was the unearthly quiet. It seemed that the darkness and the quiet blended so perfectly that it appeared impossible to walk through it. Except for the special reflectors on a mule-driver's cap, the light from the lamps gave but a feeble glow that reached only a few feet ahead. The drivers had their lamps equipped with special reflectors, and they were kept polished. These were safety precautions, protecting both driver and mule. However, miners digging coal would not polish the reflectors, because the bright light only served to cause the eyes to weaken and what light they got from the duller ones was ample for the close-up type of work.

There were millions of rats of all colors and sizes in a mine as large as was this one. They were everywhere. There were loners, pairs, and droves. There were pintos, white, brown, black, and what have you. However, strange as it may seem, those rodents would not attack a human being even when he attempted to take a nap. Many of the miners made pets of the mine rats and sold them on top. They were exceptionally clean rats—in fact they were just different in every way from the common rat except in size and looks. There were roaches, and these too were of a special variety. They grew as big as humming birds, or almost so, and they would not molest a human being in any way. On several occasions I knew of men taking one or two of these insects to his cell to destroy the bedbugs. They did a fine job and soon became a fast-moving item on the black market. These insects could also be trained, up to a certain point. I did not see it, but I read where a fellow trained a roach to go from his cell to another in the solitary cellhouse, carrying a cigarette tied to its back.

These natural denizens of the underworld were held almost sacred by the miners. Many miners owed their lives to the uncanny ability of both the mine rat and the roach to hear noises in the earth long before any sound was picked up by the human ear. When they heard these sounds, they were able to tell the severity of the condition. When they were seen leaving a room hurriedly and in numbers, it was a sure sign that a severe fall was on the way. I have never known of a case when this warning was false. They were the best insurance the miner had. It was not taken lightly when anyone deliberately killed one of these friends.

The mine was also a place where resentments slowly but surely turned to hate and viciousness. Men who normally would have been easy-going and congenial men, often permitted bitterness to rub them into a strong desire for revenge, assuming the foolish attitude, no doubt, that "Someone has to pay for this." The only time a man heard an encouraging word was when he talked to himself. This was often, but in time a man could find little encouragement for himself. He learned to hate his own life. He had little to look forward to except work and profanity, toil and sweat, blood and suffering. Up and down—routine over and over again each long and miserable day. He had no incentive to do a good job, just enough to keep from being punished. He received the same treatment for a good job or a mediocre one, and efficiency did not open a door to anything better.

Every day was a fight to get honest weights for his coal, or to keep some drone who was handy with a pen from stealing it from him. He never knew a moment away from danger of some sort—falling coal or rock, or perhaps the wrath of some other convict who had gone berserk. The mine was the breeding place of corruption, perversion, and discouragement.

Most of the work in a mine was done lying down, sometimes in mud and water with a constant threat of a gas explosion imminent. The stubborn, hard-packed earth had to be hacked out from beneath the coal vein so that the coal could be wedged down, broken up, turned over and over for the thirty or forty feet to the loading boards,* and loaded into cars for the trip to the scales. Moving of the coal in this manner, which was known as rustling, was done in one of two ways. The miner could lie on his side, sometimes in mud and water, and throw the coal back over his head, operating with a small, short-handled shovel, which was called a rustling shovel or a gob shovel. The only other way was for the miner to sit with his legs folded beneath him and with his head almost between his ankles, scooping the coal ahead of him. If a man was able to rustle ten cars of coal in a day, he was a celeb-

---

* Planks put down in an entry to shovel from.

rity known as a "ten-car rustler." All of these I ever knew
could be counted on one hand with fingers to spare.

All mine guards were known as bosses. The pit boss was
the top man, followed by the mule boss and the lowly but
important division boss. Fire bosses could be any guards who
were willing to come in about 4:30 A.M. every work day and
crawl the face with a safety lamp to determine where the largest concentrations of gas had formed during the previous
night. At each "division board"* there was a bulletin slate
with the number of each room in that division written on it.
When the fire boss found gas in a place, he would mark it on
this slate. If a man found one *x* in front of his room number,
he knew that there was a trace of gas and that he would have
to be careful until it cleared later in the day. If there were two
x marks for his room, there was enough gas that the miner
should not go in with his light on his head—"Hold it close to
the floor—gas forms at the ceiling"; if three *x*'s showed, "Do
not take light into room"; if four, "Stay out until further
orders."

There were certain safety rules—most of which were ignored—aimed at preventing miners from being seriously
burned. A man working at the coal vein was supposed to always wear a shirt. The gas always hung in the roof of the
room. If it happened to be ignited and the miner was alert
enough to fall flat and lie still, the chances were great that he
would not be burned severely if he had a shirt on. The worst
mistake a miner could make was to try and outrun the flames.
The vacuum in this tight place caused the flames to be pulled
behind anything moving, and it almost always caught up unless the victim was lucky enough to beat it to an air-course
door. These doors were usually about ten-feet square and
very thick. They directed the flow of air so that the men at
the face were always in a draft. If ignited gas hit one of these

---

* A large blackboard at division headquarters on which orders were written.

doors while moving and before burning itself out, there was always an explosion and the door was usually demolished. However, if no one was running in front of it, causing the vacuum to give it added speed, it would almost always turn off at a dead entry* and dissipate. There were many ways in which a man could be burned, and the following is one of the strangest and most humorous, if we can count any misfortune humorous.

It was customary in some divisions to use an empty carbide can for a latrine. This was so that it could be hauled away each night and destroyed. The cans always had a few pounds of powdered carbide left in the bottom of the can, and in this powder were usually many live crystals of this explosive. We had just posted a new can one morning when I noticed a young Mexican boy sit down with his old newspaper for a few minutes of relief and pleasure. Everything seemed all right for a few minutes, and the sitter was a perfect picture of re-laxation—that is, until, for some reason he ducked his head, directing the flame on his head to point downward. Then, up jumped the devil**—and the youth. There was a loud roar, the flames shot the boy right off the seat, and he took off run-ning, screaming like a banshee and trying to hold his pants up with one hand while he fanned with the paper. This was a terrible thing to laugh about, but I did, even as I was trying to shout instructions to the injured man. We finally got him stopped, and found that he was seriously burned, but not fa-tally. He came out of the hospital several months later in good health but with a scar that would keep him from win-ning a "perfect body" contest.

The mine was the one place where work was spelled with a big *W* and where the only appreciation shown was the privi-lege—if it can rightly be called that—of doing it over and over,

* An entry leading to a room that has been abandoned.
** Prison expression meaning "here came trouble."

day after day, until it seemed at times that there was no use going any further. There was no end to the coal vein, nor the callousness to which the men who dug it were subjected. It was a whirligig of misery and unrequited hard labor with no reward except the right to partake of the meager fare that was the daily menu and a smelly bunk on which to try and rest at night, while the vermin and other pests did their best to see that the effort was a failure. Sleep came only with total exhaustion.

To merely say that this sort of life was body-wrecking and soul-searing would not tell the story as it really was. It is difficult to explain how the men endured so much for so little.

The life in the mines became so hopeless to many men that they resorted to self-mutilation in order to escape just for a short time the monotonous routine and the frustrations. Many young men crippled themselves for life so that they might be removed from the certain fate of becoming perverts. They were the ones who could not desert their inbred pride even in a desperate situation. But I must confess that the ones who were of this calibre were pitifully few. These self-harming procedures for getting out of work were called bugging. There were many of them, and all were used at one time or another. The one most commonly tried first was one which promised no danger to the man permanently—neither did it promise success in the quest. It did not always work.

The first thing the convict had to do was to get a needle and a hair from a mule's tail. He threaded the needle with the hair, pinched up the skin over a joint and drove the needle through both layers. He then clipped the hair off close to the skin on both sides, leaving a piece of hair under the skin. When the skin was released, this small piece of hair would, if everything went well, work its way down into the joint, causing severe swelling with little or no pain. A swelling, especially around the knee joint, was good for several days' lay-in. The symptom was one common to "miner's knee."* However, if the doctor should suspect self-mutilation, and so stated, woe be unto that man. This happened occasionally.

Some of the methods resulted in death simply because the user did not know of the dangers involved. Yet, I heard many say that they would rather be dead than to continute under those conditions. Another way to get out of work was to cut a small gash on a knuckle, or between the fingers, and fill the gash with lye or some other caustic material such as carbide. In a few minutes this would burn a large section of flesh around the area. After it was well cooked, the burnt flesh was dug out with a knife, and this left a running sore—good for several days, if the man could explain how it happened to the doctor's satisfaction.

Other men used cruder methods, and these were the ones that usually ended in death or permanent injury. I have witnessed men stand by the track as a trip of coal went by, and suddenly stick a foot or hand under the wheels, permitting several loaded cars to pass over the member; and I never heard one make a sound as it happened. It was a more or less common occurrence for men to drive a pick through a foot or leg, and once, at least, a man drove one through both feet. He admitted it, and told the prison officials, "You can't do a damn thing about it. I'm crippled for life." But he was wrong. They did do something about it. They treated him until the danger was past, then put him in the tailor shop on a "punishment" task. This meant that he was required to produce somewhat more work than the regular task, and he could not earn anything until such a time as the officials felt like letting bygones be bygones—and the officials were not a compassionate lot.

One of the more drastic methods was to inject some foreign

* A swelling of the knee joint caused by crawling on the hard, rough floor of a mine.

substance under the skin, causing infection. By some strange act of Providence, many men got away with this, but I knew of one who died a horribly painful death. He injected disinfectant into his leg. At first it just made him ill; then the leg had to be taken off at the knee, and later at the hip. This was as far as they could go, and it wasn't far enough. He lay for weeks and suffered until death came. This ended that practice. I never again heard of anyone trying the same trick. These are a few of the many things tried by men who found the going too rough.

When I arrived at my division, I was met by the boss, a man named Bill Marchefsky. Bill was an old-time coal digger and a fine fellow. He asked me, "Have you ever dug coal before?" I didn't want to seem like a pantywaist, so I said, "Yeah, I've dug a lot of coal." I think he knew I was lying. He had a sort of "We'll see" grin on his face. But he said, "Fine, I'll give you a room by yourself. I got one down here that needs opening up. I always put experienced men in these dangerous places."

"Oh-oh," I thought, "I've let my big mouth pick up a bigger load than my hips can carry." And that is just what I had done. He left me alone in what is called a double butt.* I had no idea whether I should take the top off and pull the coal out, or take the bottom out and break it off. I was in a real jam. I crept up on that place like a wild Indian spotting a wagon train and looked both ways. All I saw was darkness— and lots of it. I was sitting, trying to figure a way out of my dilemma, when I noticed a pile of big black chunks all piled up neatly beside the loading boards. I thought, "Boy, am I lucky? Whoever had this room before has gone off and left a lot of coal all ready to load."

I worked like a slave for the next hour, and when I had finished, I had two fine cars to send out. I put my room tag

---

* A mine room that is blocked at both ends.

on them and decided I had earned a nap. When I went out at bumps* the boss said, "You must be a real coal digger. The book says you sent out two loads. That is the most I ever saw taken out of a double butt in that short time." I strutted around like a pouter pigeon. I had it made.

When we got to the top, the mine superintendent was waiting for the boss—and me. He said, "You sure did all right for a beginner. Those were real big loads."

"Yeah, I could have done better," I said, "but I didn't want to overdo it the first day."

He looked at me for a moment, then he looked like he was about to have a stroke. "You DID overdo it, you damned idiot! Don't you know coal from black sulphur? Those cars weighed five thousand pounds apiece. You can't get that much coal on one of them. I ought to put you in the hole. I would, only I can see you are a moron." I started to say something, and he screamed, "Shut your big mouth—you're just fixing to tell a damn big lie anyhow." I wondered how he knew.

Next morning, Bill said, "Well, Hardrock, you gave such a fine exhibition of mining, I have decided to promote you to a job that don't take much brawn, but lots of brains. I figure that anyone who is as big a liar as you are should be able to handle it." He told me that from then on I was a pusher. A pusher is a man who distributes the empty cars and keeps track of the loaded ones sent out of each room. Right away my nimble brain saw the possibilities involved in this new position. I could sell empty cars to the highest bidder and make a small fortune—I thought. How could I have known that I was walking right into another jam?

I scouted around and found out—or thought I found out—who I could safely steal cars from, and who would buy them. I got an order for three empties off the first trip. The rule was

* Quitting time.

that men who had not yet loaded out their task had first call on the cars. But this was a small item as far as I was concerned. I knew I could handle any trouble that might come up. So when the trip came in, I took three cars and gave them to my client. As I started to leave, he asked me who I took the cars from. I told him and he gave me a funny look. He said, "Are you sure you know what you're doing?" I assured him that I did, and went on about my business. When I came to the switch where I had taken the cars from, the man was there. He said, "Has there been a trip in yet?"

"Yes, but you'll have to wait until the next trip for your cars, I had another place for them."

"But I haven't got my task out yet. I need those cars. He was very calm—and nice.

"Sorry, you'll just have to wait," I said, rather nonchalantly.

"Listen," he said, and his voice had changed considerably, "three of those cars were mine. I want them on this switch in one hour. If they ain't here, I'm coming looking for them—and you." He turned and walked away.

I went back to the man who had gotten the cars and told him what had transpired. I pretended I wasn't worried about it, but when he finished telling me about the other man, I quit pretending. This man was one of the most dangerous men in the mine. He had killed two men and hurt several others. By the time I had pushed three empty cars weighing about three thousand pounds from another division about a mile away, where I had stolen them, I had decided to quit the car racket.

I had plenty of reason to think I had decided right. A short time later I witnessed my first killing. I have wished many times it had been my last. It happened over a piece of coal that was not worth five cents and really belonged to no one. Reed Boley and Carl Helms had been friends since childhood. They were always found together and hardly ever disagreed on anything. One noon, just before the dinner bumps, Carl had been away from his room for a few minutes. As he returned, he saw Reed taking a piece of coal off the line prop.* It appeared to him that it had been lying on his side. He called to Carl and said, "You're getting a little too far to my side there, buddy."

"What do you mean?" Carl called back. "That coal was on my side of the line."

"No, it was on my side, and I don't want you taking my coal. You put it back, or there is going to be trouble."

"I'm not putting it back, and no one is going to take it." Carl was angry.

"If it ain't back when I get back from dinner, I'll get it or kill you," Reed replied as he left the room.

This happened on a day when the dull picks were taken to the dinner board to be sent to the top for sharpening. Carl took one with him as he left for dinner. As he reached the board and walked past Reed, who was sitting down, Reed said, "I'll get you, you son of a bitch."

Carl whirled and drove the pick into Reed's chest. He said, "You're too late, I done got you." Reed died in a few minutes.

Carl was tried for this murder and given a life sentence. He seemed to be repentant, behaved himself for several years, then applied for clemency, and his sentence received a bottom of twenty years. He worked hard, educated himself, and was eventually granted a parole. He went to California and opened a machine shop, and the last report I had was that he was married and had two fine children.

During one of my brief excursions into the free world, I happened to be in Santa Rosa, California. I was walking down the street one day, and I heard someone call my name. I looked into the street, and a pickup truck was standing there and the driver was motioning for me to come out. I went out, and who was the driver but Carl. He insisted I come home

_____
* A wooden prop set on a line dividing rooms.

with him and meet the family. I went and was never more surprised in my life. It was a beautiful home, and a beautiful woman met us at the door with two little towheads peeking around her apron. It was Carl's wife and two children.

As the evening wore on, nothing was ever said about Lansing or what happened there; but later I had a chance to talk with Carl alone, and the subject came up. I said, "Carl, we were always good friends, and I have often wondered what happened between you and Reed down there." He studied a moment, and then is when I realized for the first time that it is the contagious disease called fear that permeates every man from the time he walks in that gate until he leaves—and sometimes after he leaves. He said, "Les, you know that in that place when a man threatens you, it is automatic that it be taken seriously. The truth of the matter is, I was afraid—and yet, now that I have had time to think, I realize that it was just bluff on Reed's part. I haven't slept well one night since it happened, and if there was any way that I could undo what has been done, I would gladly do it and Reed would be welcome in my home."

The next killing happened over a misplaced car of coal, and it happened so fast and unexpectedly that I hardly had time to get sick, as I always did when I saw these things.

I was standing, talking with a friend, when we noticed two men standing off to one side. They seemed to be in a mild argument, but it didn't seem to be anything serious. Suddenly one shouted, "That car of coal is mine. I don't give a damn if you had one on the trip or not. But there's just one way you'll get it, and that is to kill me."

The other man turned as if to walk away, saying, "All right, if that is how you want it." Suddenly he whirled and plunged a ten inch blade into the other man's heart, killing him almost instantly, but not before he managed to blurt out, "Why?" The killer stooped over and stuck his victim four more times.

A few minutes later a pusher came in and said, "I found

that car of coal. It was misplaced when the trip got off the track, and the numbers got switched." The killer shrugged his shoulders when he heard this, looked down at his victim, and said, "So what? He put the idea in my head. And anyhow, he had more time than he could do. I just helped him do it." He was never tried, but was later killed himself by someone who knew his reputation and took no chances.

I decided I would give up the job I had. It was too dangerous and tempting. I knew I was a pushover for a fast buck, and as long as I was close to that temptation I was in danger. I began pulling strings for a job in the mule barn. I had been around mules and horses all my life, and I liked them. I figured this would be the ideal spot for me to do my bit.* When I finally got the transfer and became a relief driver, I was as contented as a man can be in a prison. It was on this job that I spent several of the most exciting and educational years of my life.

* Term or sentence.

Mine Mules

And the iron gin that waits for Sin
Had caught us in its snare.

I soon learned that environment is not only an important factor in the lives of human beings, but that it also brought out the good and bad in animals. If either man or beast is possessed of admirable qualities which have heretofore failed to show, the prison coal-mine environment surely brought them to the surface. On the other hand, if a seemingly intelligent and congenial man or mule had a hidden streak of viciousness or cheapness, it also found its way into view.

I did well on my new job and soon became a trouble-shooter. I was sent out to help other drivers who were having difficulty with their mules. I broke in new mules when they came to the mine, and I was permitted to travel all over the mine at will. Because of this, I knew about everything that went on. It might be said that I was a roving reporter for the miner's edition of the "grapevine telegraph." I became well acquainted with all the mules, each of which had an interesting story of his own. Several of these animals had spent thirty years underground, while others were fortunate enough to come up and spend their last days in the fresh air and grass. One of these latter became a much-publicized and colorful character—the most famous of all mine mules—Old Jim.

I have a vivid recollection of the wintry morning in 1930 when Jim made his first appearance in the mine. There are many reasons why this stands out in my memory, but the main one is that it was my job to meet him and take him off the cage. The mules were always brought down on the airshaft on a specially constructed safety door. I had two helpers with me, and as we awaited Old Jim's arrival, we discussed the many things we had heard about him—things not good, but not too bad. He was reported to be capricious and very stubborn, even for a mule. It was a question as to whether we could work him at all in the mine. Many thought we couldn't; we thought we could. Only time was to tell who was right and who was wrong. But Old Jim became a legend here and gained national recognition at the time of his death on the night of September 14, 1966. He was at least fifty years of age, as nearly as we could reckon it.

When the cage arrived and was put down softly, we began pounding at the bar which held the door, so we could open it. Every time we struck once, Jim struck twice with both feet. After each barrage he would bray louder, then look over the side to see if he was making an impression. As soon as we got the door down, I ducked in beside him and said, "Get over, Jim. Don't make me wallop you." I was promptly told—in mule language—where I could go and how long I could stay. I just barely slid under those flying hooves, and then I did get angry. I moved up to the middle of his body out of the way of those nimble feet. I thought if I could stay there he wouldn't be able to get a good shot at me. I had failed, however, to reckon with Jim's uncanny ability to meet unexpected situations. He immediately moved to the other side with his feet and leaned with all his weight upon me. I was pinned and knew that for the moment it was a stalemate. I figured I would do better to talk myself out of this one rather than try to bully this smarty. I thought for a moment that he was falling for my soft line of talk, when one of my helpers untied the halter rope. Jim immediately lunged out the door and took off up the entry. Right then began one of the biggest mule hunts in prison history.

For a mule that had never been in a mine before, Jim sure knew how to find his way around. It was pitch dark—for him —as he turned south and went toward number four division. We called for them to watch for him, and we closed in. We got to the division, but they had not seen the runaway. He had hid in a deserted entry somewhere and let us go past. We called the bottom and told the men at the mule barn to stop Jim. The man who answered said, "You're just a shade late. Something went past about a minute ago, and I think it was him." We finally hemmed him up in another part of the mine, and all the way back to the barn, all Jim did was bray.

This mule always seemed to be laughing at us. We soon found out that he wasn't mean, just ornery and full of life. He had his own ideas about how much work he should do, and that was all he had any intentions of doing. I have seen him stand and kick until he was ready to drop from exhaustion, rather than pull one extra car of coal. Four was his limit, and he learned to count the bumps when the slack was taken up. If there were more than three bumps, he would take about two steps, turn and look over his shoulder, then let fly with both feet. If he was lucky enough to kick the tailchain* loose, he was gone. And, believe it or not, he could find his way to the barn in the pitch darkness—sometimes several miles.

Jim soon became everyone's pet. He would beg for a chew of tobacco or anything else he could get. He liked bread and syrup, and it was customary for the miners to take a piece to him as they went back to work from the "dinner board."** It

* A short chain used to pull cars, reaching from the butt stick (short single-tree fastened to the traces) to a hook on the front of the car.
** A small board held on the knees, from which food is eaten.

finally got to where those who neglected this little courtesy found it a bit difficult to get past. He had a remarkable memory for anyone who treated him badly or forgot him. He could spot a new man a mile away. How he knew they were newcomers, we never could figure out. He would always put on a special act for them by laying his ears back, switching his tail, and stomping his feet as if he intended to commit mayhem. If they handed him a piece of tobacco or bread, he would calm down, throw up his ears, and grin that infernal mule grin and almost get mushy.

Jim, like most mules, could open a door on the move—that is, if he was moving the way the door opened. He would merely bump it with his nose and slither through, then the cars would catch it until the trip was through. He got so he could open it the other way when there was no trip following. We put small strips of canvas on the door for handles. He would take these strips in his mouth, throw his head quickly, then jump through the opening. He began doing this and running off to the barn so often that we had to take the handles off.

Jim worked in the mines until they were sealed up in 1947. He was then brought to the top and went into semiretirement. He roamed around and occasionally pulled a small water wagon until his death in 1966. Old Jim was at least fifty years old at that time. He was mourned by all who knew him and many outside who had only heard of him. At that time the prison magazine, *The Stretch*, had this to say: Charley O, the mascot of the Kansas City A's baseball team is perhaps the most pampered mule in history, but the abundance of affection bestowed upon him could not possibly be of greater quality than that which another of his breed has received from inmates here for many years. He was possessed of a personality streaked with meanness, but modified with loveable loyalty to prisoners with whom he worked, and by demonstrations of gratitude to those who tended him when his work day was over."

I, who knew Jim longer than any other person at the Lansing prison, felt his death as a personal blow. At that time I wrote in the prison magazine:

It leaves a feeling that only one who has shared the dangers and fears of a prison coal mine can feel for a companion. It recalls to mind the many disagreements we had, and the sometimes humorous, sometimes serious outcome of these disputes.

It brings back the picture of the old rascal, frisking a miner's pocket for candy or a chew of tobacco, and refusing to let him by if he failed to produce. It brings back memories of the stable at the end of the long day when differences were forgotten and forgiven and Jim gave a friendly nudge, and received in return an extra measure of grain stolen from the grainery.

Jim was a rogue, a thief, and all around bounder who won many hearts with his antics, both in the mines and out.

In the prison mines it was customary to slam the big doors in the air course as a signal to quit work and assemble at the end of the day. This signal was called "bumps" and was recognized by the mules as well as the men. Sometime during the night of September 14, old Jim heard "bumps" for the last time. Only this time it was the gate to the "big corral" where old mine mules assemble when their earthly task is finished.

Judging from the condition of the turf where Jim's body was found, he protested as he always did something he didn't want. We hope in Jim's new home the clover is shoulder high. We send him off as we received him so many years ago. With admiration and best wishes.

There was a fierce bond of loyalty between the miners and the mine mules—a closeness that would hardly be noticed anywhere else. They had much in common. Both were prisoners, sentenced to hard labor and subject to the same treatment. Each had a certain amount of work to do, which the state demanded in payment for bed, board, and their sins. It seemed that these animals realized that the prisoners were their only friends, and the convict realized that his life was often dependent on his mule. It was a natural understanding, and yet rather strange. It was a serious offense to mistreat any mule, and especially someone else's mule. Many men have been badly injured because of this.

Another celebrity was Star. He was a hill mule. The hill mules were specialists, and the stories about them are the most fantastic and exciting. Star's driver was a lifer and was also a very good friend of mine. He had a toothbrush hid away in the mine, and he would manage to get down early every morning and brush Star's teeth and polish his hooves. He took a lot of ribbing about it, but he didn't mind. He was serious. He really thought the world of Star. One morning a guard happened to catch him at his chores. He stood and watched for a minute, then said, "You take better care of that mule than I do my family."

My friend looked at him for a moment, then replied, "I don't doubt that a damn bit, and this mule probably thinks more of me than your family does of you." Then he ducked a left hook and took out running. He knew he was in a world of trouble. Just as he disappeared around a curve, the guard was standing in the middle of the track throwing rocks at him. This caper cost him a long stay in number two cellhouse, which was the isolation house. My friend would have stayed longer, but hill drivers are not made overnight and he was needed, so got a break.

In order to understand the skills needed by both driver and mule on a hill run, it is necessary to picture a hill beneath the ground. The hills were very deceiving both in length and steepness. They were all narrow, and in places both the driver and mule had to duck their heads in order to pass in safety. The regular travelers got to know just exactly where each of these places was located by a landmark a certain distance before. There were special caretakers to keep the hills free from rocks and other debris, but like all workers in a prison, most of them cared little for the lives of others and were apt to neglect this important job, making it doubly dangerous. Such carelessness accounted for the death of several drivers and mules, but it was difficult to prove, and no one was ever blamed.

Hill Number 1 handled all the coal coming from divisions one, two, and eleven. The divisions were located near or beneath the Missouri River and were always wet and muddy. Pumps were kept busy twenty-four hours a day, and still the men worked in water that came close to covering them as they lay on their side to work. Outside these divisions was a park, a widened spot with double rails where the cars were assembled into trips and prepared for transfer to the loading cage. The park had two sets of tracks. One for the loads, and one for the empties. When there were enough cars to make a trip, Star pulled them over the brink of Number 1 Hill. He ran in front of them until they were rolling free, and when he came to a small niche which had been cut out of the rib, or sidewall, he jumped into it. There was just enough room for him to squeeze in and let the rolling trip pass him.

This maneuver required precision timing, and a slip on the part of the driver or mule would have meant certain disaster to both. There was no light except the faint beam which came from the lamp worn by the driver. If he failed to hold his head just right, the flame was extinguished by the rushing air. This did happen many times, but a good hill mule would keep on his course until the driver, who was a wizard with that light, snatched off the cap and hit the flint wheel again. The mules had an uncanny way of knowing about where they were at all times—sometimes when the driver was in doubt. The mule seemed to know that to falter meant sure death.

As the mule reached the niche in the wall, the driver gave a quick kick at the tail chain, jumping to the niche at the same time. If he happened to slip as he jumped, it was "Katy, bar the door." It was all over for them both.

Star would crouch in this niche, pulling his body in to avoid the cars. He would stand perfectly still until he could tell by the rumbling of the trip that it had gone. He would then relax, wait for the dust to clear, then turn and trudge slowly back up the hill, tossing his head as if saying, "I wonder when that trip will finally get me?" He found out just the day before the final run was to be made by a mule. The electric trolley was to take over the next day.

On that fatal day, Star's regular driver was sick and a relief man took his place. They made one trip without incident. But the other drivers knew that the relief man had been drinking, and advised him not to go. He replied that he could do it all right. One of the drivers told me later that as Star went over the crest, he hesitated as if he didn't want to go. However, the cars had begun to roll, and he had no choice. When he came to the break-off point, the driver either kicked at the chain and missed, or never made an attempt. The result was that Star was pulled between the heavy cars and the rib and was literally mangled. The trip buckled, and the driver was crushed beneath it. When he was dug out, an empty and broken whiskey bottle was found in his pocket.

We loaded Star's body in a car and took it to the top. It was standing on a siding in the yard when the men came up. They had to pass this car as they left the shower and walked toward the gate. I noticed that not one man looked at Star, and not a man left his cap on as he passed. The miners paid tribute to a friend and fellow prisoner.

Number 48 Hill was the longest in the mine, but was not as steep as some others. Number 1 and Number 48 were separated by a distance of about one hundred yards of flat floor. When the cars reached the bottom of Number 1 Hill they were picked up by another famous hill mule named Speck. The procedure was about the same, except that Speck had a somewhat larger place in which to hide and he had a little more time in which to get out of the way. He could outrun the cars to this point and not be rushed. But any of these hill mules could, in an emergency, operate on any hill.

The next mule in line was Rock, called the Switch Engine. He picked up the trip at the bottom of Number 48 Hill and pulled it through the high place* to the terminal, where it was loaded and sent to the top. Rock was a strange mule. He was a loner and a killer when given the least reason. He had killed one driver and crippled several. He did his work. He accepted no favors from anyone and wanted nothing to do with anyone except in the line of duty. He seldom kicked, but when he did, he did it with murder in his heart. He was a marksman and seldom had to take more than one shot. His driver had to be on the alert every minute. He behaved well; in fact, he moved around as if he was lazy or half asleep, but he was neither. I knew several drivers who tried in every way to make friends with Rock, but it was no soap.

There was Toby, the one-man mule. Only two men ever had much luck working Toby in the mine. One was a fellow named Clem Kier, and the other was myself. He would pull his heart out for either of us, but for anyone else he was a problem. After about ten years he had to be brought out. He would wander about the yard on top, where he had his own pasture and did fine until it rained. When the raindrops began to hit his back, he almost went crazy. He thought it was slate dripping from the room. This usually precedes a fall in the mine, and all mules knew it.

Tom was the oldest mule in the mine. He had been down at least thirty years when I went to the mines. He had lost all his hair and was as slick as a billiard ball. I never knew Tom to take a day off other than the weekends. He was slow, but more dependable than any other mule in the mine.

Mike was killed in the mines as the result of his own stub-

* A place where the roof had fallen, leaving a 40-foot hole above.

bornness and flighty nature. I felt very badly about his death, as I was driving him at the time it happened.

It was bumps, and I had started out of Number 5 Division with the last trip of the day. It consisted of six cars of coal and slate. It was customary for me to always leave the big door open and hooked back when I went in, because it was at the bottom of a short hill. If for any reason I failed to get the trip stopped and properly spragged, there would be a terrible smash-up if this door was closed, because it opened toward the trip.

When I returned, I did get the trip stopped at the top of the hill, but could find no sprag. As I walked back to the front of the trip, I saw someone's light at the door. I had a feeling that the door was being released, and I shook my head, signalling in the negative. At that moment, Mike moved out. I heard the door boom, and I jumped on the tail chain and tried to get enough slack so that I could unhook the chain and throw it under the wheels to wreck the trip. I couldn't get it loose because Mike, now thoroughly frightened, kept it tight. I jumped off and began running backward in the middle of this irregular roadway. I kept trying to sooth Mike and at the same time get the chain free. However, it was no use. I looked over my shoulder and saw the door very close. I took a head-long dive over the first car and waited. I had no sooner hit the top than I knew the worst had happened. I crawled down and saw Mike pinned to the door. He was bent double and looked pitiful. The terrific jar had derailed two cars of slate, and nothing could be done until those cars were put back on the track. It happened that a group of miners were coming up behind me, and they broke a record getting those cars back on the rail. This was quite a project under the best conditions. As the cars were rolled back, Mike fell to the ground. I went to him and took his tail and lifted. "Come on, Mike," I said, "I know you can get up." He did get up and walked 1200 feet to the park before he fell again for the last time. He tried gamely to get up, but his hind quarters would not function. I sat down and held his head in my lap and petted him. He looked up at me as if to say, "It's all right, pal. These things happen."

The veterinarian came and said that we would have to destroy Mike. He told me to get a hammer. I told him to go to hell and walked away to a little shack down the track—where I confess, I shed tears of which I was not ashamed. I still wake up in the night and shudder when I think of what could have happened to me if I had stumbled that day. And I know that if it was possible for Mike to speak to me now, he would say, "You did your best."

Strange things happened in the mines. I have been told by guards and convicts that there are men who are still there, who were covered and never found. Anyone who knows mines realizes that this could have happened. And yet, men have stood at the scene of a thousand-car fall and never got a scratch.

5

Prison
Friendships

For none can tell to what red Hell
His sightless soul may stray.

EVERY MAN gives reasons why he committed the acts that sent him to prison. However, these reasons are usually subterfuge used because the man himself doesn't know the deep-down reasons. In some men these things become manifest after they have lain dormant for years—sometimes since childhood. The sudden urge to seek relief from the inner turmoil perhaps becomes so strong that the man, who is perhaps weak to begin with, has no defense mechanism which he can muster quickly enough to handle the situation. Maybe it is caused by an old hurt that has festered and become unbearable; and perhaps the cause of that hurt really meant very little in the beginning. But as resentments are permitted to grow, little things become very big—too big for the usually unstable criminal mind to cope with properly.

One of the things that is most effective in producing bitterness and hatred is false accusation. This is true in domestic affairs just as it is in criminal action. One of the best cases I recall as an example of this is the case of Willie Sells. However, Willie was strong enough to reason things out in a rational way, and he did not become infected with hate and

70

bitterness, although he had every reason to do so. His story should help everyone remember, no matter who you are or what your station in life, it could happen to you.

In 1885 Willie Sells was a frail sixteen-year-old boy living on a farm near Erie, Kansas, with his parents and an older brother and sister. The Sells family was not wealthy, nor could they be termed poor. They made a comfortable living, and while they were considered a rather odd family, they managed to get along with the folks around them. Willie was a dreamer, but he was also a good worker and had never been in any trouble. He told me the following story several years before his death in Kansas City.

Willie was awakened in the night by a commotion that seemed to come from the room where his parents and his sister slept. He slipped out of bed and looked in through a partially opened door. He was horrified to see two large, bearded strangers hacking at his parents with hatchets. The men saw him and quickly ran past him into the yard, where they mounted horses and rode away. The frightened boy managed to pull himself together and ran to the nearest neighbor's house for help. He awakened the family and told them that his parents and sister had been killed.

After summoning several other neighbors, they returned to the Sells farm, where they found just what Willie said they would, except that in the same bed where Willie had been sleeping, they also found the body of Willie's brother. When asked why he had not mentioned his brother, Willie said that he hadn't even known that his brother was home; he had been away at school, and must have come in after Willie had gone to sleep. This story seemed weak to the police, and Willie was arrested and charged with first-degree murder. He was quickly brought to trial—if it could be called that—and convicted. He was sentenced to serve life at hard labor in the Kansas State Penitentiary at Lansing.

It was several years before a lady in Kansas City, Kansas,

became interested in Willie and believed his story. Her father, who was a prominent jurist, agreed to help her, and they set out to prove that the boy was railroaded. This started one of the most interesting and revealing investigations ever conducted in Kansas, and exposed a gross miscarriage of justice.

Trained investigators talked with the neighbors who had been at the farm on that dreadful night. Nearly all of these admitted that upon entering the house, they had noticed a strong odor of chloroform. Willie had mentioned this, although he didn't know what it was. This had never been mentioned at the trial. When asked why, the people said, "They didn't ask." Other folks stated they had seen horse droppings near the spot where Willie had said the horses stood. They, too, said they had not been asked. It was soon discovered that few if any of these witnesses had ever been subpoenaed. The ones who were, it was found, were carefully questioned in order to bring out the answers wanted, not necessarily the facts.

The druggist in town said that he had sold a bottle of chloroform to two bearded strangers on the night of the murders, and that he saw them ride away in the direction of the Sells farm. He said he later also had found the bottle in which he had put the chemical in the weeds on the Sells farm, which he had bought after Willie's conviction. He said that he had not been called upon to testify, nor had he been asked anything.

After years of investigation the results were taken to governor after governor, all of whom said that even though it seemed that the boy was innocent, they would not take the responsibility of ordering his release. But at last a governor was elected who placed justice above political aspiration. His name was Hoch, and in 1907 he granted Willie Sells a full pardon. He had served twenty-one years for a crime he did not commit.

In talking with me, Willie admitted that his inability to tell about his brother was a strong factor in the circumstantial evidence upon which he had been convicted. He was not bitter—or if he was, he hid it from me. He said he guessed it was just "one of those things." He was, of course, very grateful to those who did believe in him and for the fact that he was able to learn pharmacy while working in the prison hospital. He followed this profession after his release from prison. We discussed the possibilities of what may have happened on that night so long ago and came up with the following conclusion.

It had long been thought that Mr. Sells had money hidden on the farm, and the strangers were looking for it. The men, being frightened when they saw someone looking into the room where they were committing murder, had only one thought in mind at the moment. That was to get away fast. They rode a few miles, and then realizing that they had been seen, decided they had better go back and get the one eyewitness. They came back, searched the house, and found Willie's brother, who had come home from school in another town for a short visit. They supposed that this was the one who had seen them, so they murdered him and rode away again. Willie said, "That is how it could have happened. I don't know. All I know is, I didn't do it. I had no reason to hate any of my family, and if I had, I could not have done a thing like that. I hope the telling of my story will make folks understand that anything can happen—to anyone, at any time."

Willie's friends were all elated at the action of Governor Hoch, including the prison officials. But the die-hard citizens of the vicinity where the crime was committed were not so happy. They burned both Governor Hoch and Willie Sells in effigy during a protest demonstration.

The primary difference between the law-abiding citizen and the criminal is that the normal person is content to go along patiently and work for his success and happiness—his day in the sun—while the criminal does not have the patience and forethought to reason a problem out in a sensible way. He feels that he must leap into the limelight by performing some daring—and stupid—deed. There are probably many things which cause this irrational thinking. One of the causes may be a lack of funds to live as he thinks he should live if he is to be happy. His lack of forethought is responsible for his inability to understand that there are orderly and effective ways of meeting this problem without jeopardizing his freedom.

Young Dale Jones and his accomplice, Slim Edwards, are a case in point. I knew both these men very well. In fact, I unwittingly furnished part of the equipment used in their last escapade, which resulted in their death. They were possessed of pleasing personalities and were well liked by the inmate body. They became acquainted while working in the twine plant. Dale, whose real name was Earnest Hardwick, was younger than Edwards. He was a boy who had already received more publicity than was good for him. He imagined that he was of the same caliber as his namesake, the real Dale Jones, robber, impersonator, and killer who was obsessed with a desire for grandeur and fame. But he, too, died by the gun in the hands of the law—not only he, but his young and beautiful wife who fought beside him, wielding a shotgun until the hopeless battle was over, ending two brief but colorful lives. They are buried at Carmel-by-the-Sea, California, just as they died, side by side.

Young Dale was master of nothing, but was the possessor of an overinflated ego, which led to his premature death and that of a boy who merely went along for the ride.

It was 1926, and I was transferred to the plumbing shop. Dale and Slim Edwards both were employed at the twine plant, which was but a short distance away. One day as I was preparing some pipe for another project, I looked up to see

Dale standing at the door. He asked me if I had a piece of three-eights pipe about three inches in length that I would give him. I didn't ask him what he wanted it for—we didn't ask in those days. I looked around and could not find what he wanted. I told him to come back later in the day and I would try and find what he needed. In the meantime, I found a piece of brass pipe with a beveled ridge at one end and nickel-plated. He said that it would do the job fine. I thought no more of the incident until later, when I saw this piece of pipe in a different guise.

It was about a week later during evening yard exercises that Dale and his gullible but courageous companion went to the night captain's office and took the captain prisoner with a dummy gun and knives. They wrecked the switchboard, rolled up some wire to make it look like they were electricians, and forced the official to accompany them to the tower at the northeast corner of the wall, where there was an inside door and two outside doors. As they approached the tower, the guard came out on the catwalk seeking identification. The captain, as ordered, told him that they were electricians and that he had brought them down to check the wires. The guard unbarred the door, and the trio entered.

Although it was not known at the time, this was intended to be a mass break. Twenty or thirty men were hid in the back part of the twine plant for the signal that the tower had been taken. It was planned that the two in the tower would open all gates and release anyone who cared to go. As these men crouched, waiting for the sign, the evening was shattered by a shot. There was a pause, and then another shot. The men in the twine plant broke for the yard after trying to set the twine plant afire. How this attempt failed is still a mystery. The sisal of which rope and twine are made is most explosive—but somehow it failed to ignite.

As the three principals walked up the steep steps, Dale was in the lead, followed by the captain, then Slim, who brought up the rear. When Dale was about three steps from the top, he pulled the dummy gun and lunged for the guard. However, the man was too alert. He merely tipped his holster and fired through the bottom. The bullet hit Dale in the stomach. By this time, Slim had forced the captain into the tower. He could have surrendered and not been hurt, but he elected to go all the way. He turned his back on the guard and began slashing the officer, a Mr. Monette. The guard jockeyed for position, then shot the knife-wielding Slim through the spine. After calling the office, the guard leaned over Dale and asked him, "Have I hurt you badly, Dale?"

"Yes," the wounded man replied. "You've killed me, you sonofabitch." This was true, but little did the wounded man know how much he would have to go through before death finally came. Examination showed that Slim was still alive, but mortally wounded, and Captain Monette was badly cut. However, the captain recovered and soon retired.

I was one of the men recruited to help carry the two men into the hospital. The doctor came, looked at them, and said, "There is nothing I can do for them. Take them across the street." That meant to take them to the little building that served as a morgue. The two men were still groaning and twitching when the door was locked and we left. If they were not dead, it didn't take long, for this room was ice-cold.

I have discussed the case of Slim Edwards with old-timers in an effort to find some excuse for his actions. He had served all but a short while of his sentence and would have been released legally. We could understand a man like Dale, who had more time than he could ever do, electing to gamble; but not Slim. Why, after being patient for so many years, take a hand in a game that promised less than one chance in a hundred of success? This is what makes one wonder why it is that men care so little for their freedom when they have it, and yet will risk their lives to regain it once it is lost. Was this a case of a man who wanted the spotlight—that leaping instead of waiting for his day in the sun? Was it the hope that whether or not he succeeded, he would be tagged a "bad man"—a man who dared assault the walls at Lansing? Was it that inexplainable feeling that some of us get at the thought of a challenge with the promise of possible liberty and excitement, for a few hours at least?

It is not always the criminal who fails to think properly under stress. I witnessed the following incident; and while the incident itself is not puzzling, what happened later is very much so. The victim of this wholly unnecessary killing was a good friend of mine, a boy of nineteen, doing a short sentence out of Kansas City. We both worked in the mine and celled on the same tier. The night before the tragedy, he had been called out to sign up for the draft. On his return to the cellhouse, he reached in through the bars of my cell and awakened me. I cursed him, and he went down the tier laughing. The next morning I pretended to be angry and told him not to do that stunt again. He said, "All right, I promise. I'll never do it again."

I had a call to the hospital that morning and was just returning to go to the mine when the trouble began. He and two companions had captured the Pit Boss and put him in the cage with the intentions of forcing him to take them through the back gate to freedom. However, they had failed to take into account the telephone on the bottom. As soon as they were on the way up, someone called the top and told what had happened. The cage was stopped short of the top, and they were trapped. In the meantime, the warden had arrived with an armed guard. He shouted to the men to come out. They told him that they could not get out until the cage had been raised, but that they did give up. They had no weapon except a hatchet, and they threw that out. The warden ordered the cage raised until there was about a one-foot opening, and then he turned to the armed guard and told him to shoot the trapped men. The guard opened fire, shooting blindly into the cage. It apparently made little difference that the Pit Boss was also a prisoner and in danger of being hit. However, he was not hit. One convict had part of an ear shot off, and my friend, the youngest, and no doubt the least harmful, was shot fatally. He died on arrival at the hospital.

I have given much thought to this incident in the years since it happened and have come to a partial conclusion. I knew this warden well, and I cannot believe that he gave that order seriously. The guard with him was more or less trigger-happy, and he wasted no time in complying when the warden spoke the words. I believe he wanted the trapped men to hear them, because he apparently did not understand that they could not get out of the cage. Another reason I cannot feel the warden intended to shoot the men is that not long after this the warden resigned his position rather than participate in a legal hanging. Or, perhaps, it was this incident that caused him to change from an advocate of capital punishment to one who was bitterly opposed to it.

The guard who did the shooting was later killed during an attempted crash-out through the front gate.

Sometimes when an official becomes confused, it turns out to be amusing rather than tragic, as in the following case. There was a captain of guards who had a habit of getting up in front of the inmate body at every meal and telling them what dirty so-and-so's they were. The language he used would put a mule skinner to shame. The longer he talked, the redder his face and the dirtier his language became. This was not thought too much about by the men, as they learned to expect it. But one day it was different, and everyone got a good laugh.

A traveling salesman for a shoe-machine company came to the prison to show his wares, and the captain was showing him around. During the tour someone stole the man's hat. At dinner, the captain and the salesman stood up before the assemblage. We thought, "Well, Cap is going to show off in front of the visitor—show him how he handles convicts."

Cap was all smiles, but somehow I could detect malice behind them. He began real nice, and we thought he might be having a change of heart. But suddenly, he boomed out, "And now, what I want to know is which one of you gentlemen stole this bastard's hat." He realized in a moment what he had done. He turned purple, looked at the visitor, and tried to smile; and then as the dining room guffawed, the captain and the salesman joined in—it was all they could do. They found the hat a week later in a sewer.

My next cellmate was one of the most likeable and colorful men I have ever had the privilege of knowing. He had been a problem throughout most of his life and had been, and was yet to be, much publicized. He was known as the last of the "loner" train robbers. His name was Bill LaTrasse. This incident deals with his first real step into the "big time" of crime. His last step is related in a later chapter.

LaTrasse's life was as full of excitement and thrills as anyone's I have ever read about. It was also full of sorrow and regret, not only for him, but for his mother, who, it is reported, burned a lamp in her window for many years, hoping Bill would turn back and come home. He was born in Missouri about 1883. His family, while not exactly wealthy, were comfortably fixed. Bill's mother gave him every opportunity, but he failed to take advantage of this help and love. In the end it was all wasted. Bill was not one to blame others for his mistakes. He realized his own weaknesses, and from his own story, women and drink were the main contributors to his downfall. He had a deep feeling of regret for having failed those who loved him and believed in him.

Bill had been in scrape after scrape, but until he was thirty years old nothing really serious had happened to him. In 1913 he decided to go it alone and pull a job that would make him noticed by the "wheels" in Kansas City, to rob a train single-handedly. He told me years later that this was to have been his masterpiece. As he talked with me, he paused at times and chuckled at some particularly humorous incident that he remembered having happened during the robbery. Then he would shake his head, as if it was hard for him to realize he had done such a thing.

He boarded a passenger train that ran between Kansas City and St. Joseph, after having cased the job for several weeks. He knew the country around the vicinity and saw no reason why he couldn't commit the robbery and make his escape. As the train rolled along, he fingered the gun in his pocket and kept thinking what he would do if he met with resistance. He said he knew one thing, and that was he would not shoot anyone unless he had to in defense of his own life. He said, "I believe that if someone had told me to go to hell when I told them to raise their hands, I would have given the job up and got off the train." Apparently no one else on the train believed this, because he had no trouble in relieving all of them of their money and other valuables. That is, all except one little old lady.

Bill went down the aisle hurriedly, as he had a "deadline" to make, but he was careful not to miss any loot. He came to an old lady wearing a shabby black dress and clutching a cloth purse tightly, as if it held a million dollars. "What's in the poke, lady?" She looked him right in the eye and replied, "Everything I own in this world, young man—two dollars and fifty cents."

"I was in a terrible hurry," Bill related, "but somehow I just had to ask her where she was going. She told she was on her way to Oklahoma to stay with a daughter. I told her to let me see if that was all the money she had in the purse. She handed it to me. I found a picture of a nice-looking young lady and two little kids—and two-fifty. I turned as if trying to get a better view of the picture, and as I did, I slipped a five I had just taken from the conductor into the purse and handed it back. I had to do it. I don't suppose she kept it, but I gave it in good faith."

Bill made his escape with no trouble, but his freedom was short-lived. He was captured, identified, and convicted. He came to the Kansas State Penitentiary on August 4, 1913. On the twelfth day of November, 1915, he escaped from the south-wing cellhouse, went to New York, and enlisted in the French Foreign Legion. It was while serving with this famous fighting force that he covered himself with glory during World War I. He was decorated by several nations for bravery. Among his trophies was the French Croix de Guerre, the highest honor the French nation can bestow upon a person. However, the fact remained that he was an escaped convict, and when he returned to the United States after the war, he was arrested and returned to "The Devil's Front Porch." This was on March 19, 1920.

Although Bill felt that he had not been given the consideration that he merited, he settled down and worked at his trade as a shoemaker. On December 22, 1923, Bill was granted a temporary Christmas parole. He made good on this parole and returned on time, January 5, 1924. But when given another parole in 1924, he didn't fare so well. He violated, and was again returned to Lansing on March 21, 1925. On June 3, 1931, he went out on expiration.

Things went fairly well for Bill for a time after he left here, but he soon began to drink and was almost down in the gutter. He walked into a hamburger place in Kansas City one night and held it up. He escaped with a few dollars. However, he was soon apprehended and received a sentence in the Missouri State Penitentiary. He served about two years and was released. He returned to his old stomping ground, Kansas City, and became associated with some old penitentiary acquaintances and went into the business of heisting illegal gambling games. One of his old cronies was Harry "Red" Downs—a well-known hood who had at one time been associated with the powerful and indiscriminate Pendergast organization. Harry had served a sentence in Lansing and was currently on parole from a fifty-year sentence in Missouri. He and his accomplices were apparently laboring under the false impression that it was no crime to hold up illegal games. This, however, was not the cause of their final downfall.

This little band operated around the Kansas City area and once or twice went as far as Topeka to ply their nefarious trade. They were doing pretty good, and this more than anything else was their eventual undoing.

Because of the fact that Harry Downs's life story up until now is so interesting and exciting, and Bill La Trasse's final years so tragic and sorrowful, I have concluded the story of both men in a later chapter. After reading the amazing facts, I feel sure the reader will agree that men must work hard at crime to crowd as much into life as did these two men. It will strengthen the saying that "Truth is stranger than fiction" and that crime only pays off in heartaches, sorrows, shame, and death.

Bill and I became good friends, and he taught me much about the art of doing time—and it is an art. I never heard Bill steer anyone wrong intentionally, and he was always among the first to contribute to any worthy cause. He once told me, "Some guys think I'm a hero. I ain't anything but a damn fool. I hate to see young kids idolize guys like me, thinking we did something great. If we were so smart, we wouldn't be in one of these places." He meant that too.

By 1926 things were a little better than they had been before. We had two sheets and a pillowcase—of course, not many of us had pillows, but we had the case if we ever got one. The food was a bit better and was kept cleaner, but the place was still a hellhole and full of bitterness, viciousness, and perversion. It was these sheets and pillowcases that were the cause of the first mine strike, which was not too bad, thanks to bad timing on the part of the instigators. But it was bad enough.

The trouble began when the sheets and pillowcases failed to get back from the laundry in time to be distributed. The convicts howled and banged on the bars all night and raised a general rumpus. However, when morning came they seemed docile enough. They went to breakfast, then went to the mine top as usual. After they were all down, the ringleaders rounded up all the bosses and took them to the mule barn. The older and better-liked ones were allowed to make hay pallets and rest on the rolling hole.* The others were made to stand in the stalls with halters on. The plan was to let all the dinner cars get down, then to block the cage so no one could get up or down. However, somebody goofed, and after the first car came down, they blocked the cage. It was then that the officials on top knew that something was wrong. They met the problem simply by closing the shaft. This made the food problem very acute, and before it was over, the convicts were trying to boil mule oats and eat them. When this didn't work, some idiot proposed killing a mule. This caused a real uproar, and the idea was abandoned.

The men stayed down three days and did a good job of tearing the mine up. Meanwhile the ringleaders were trying to get concessions from the warden. He told them that if they would come up, he would discuss their grievances. They told him they wanted him to publish in the paper that he would give them this and that. He told them to go to hell. He also added that if one officer was hurt, he would see that the men paid a terrible price. None was hurt, but a few were humiliated. At last the majority overruled the ringleaders, and the strike ended.

The leaders were weeded out and put into solitary confinement, and the rest had to go back and clean up the mess that had been made. This ended mine trouble until 1927, when another strike was staged for the privilege of being permitted

* A pen where the mules could roll and exercise.

to smoke cigarettes. This was a somewhat more serious strike than was the first, but no one was badly hurt. The mine was pretty well torn up—that is, timbers were taken down and a few rooms were pulled in.

After a few days the deputy warden warned the men that unless they surrendered and came up, he was coming down after them. They knew this deputy warden wasn't just talking, so they decided to set fires. This was their undoing. The air courses filled with smoke, and everyone was having a hard time breathing. Then to top it off, after someone had released the main cage, the deputy came down with a machine gun. He fired a burst through the double doors, and that ended the strike.

This time the ringleaders were put on a top tier in the east wing, where wire enclosures had been erected. They remained there for a long time on solitary basis. This was the last strike of any consequence in the Kansas State Penitentiary.

The damage done in these strikes contributed to the danger of the already condemned mine, and in 1947 it was closed for all time and is now sealed up. The closing of the mine removed a work hell, but it also worked hardship on both officials and convicts. The administration was faced with the problem of keeping the men occupied, and the prisoners lost their source of earning extra money. However, in later years those problems were partly solved. Only the memories of the old mine are left for the old-timers to share with the younger men.

6

The Brickyard
and the
Power Plant

And by all forgot, we rot and rot,
With soul and body marred.

THE MINE was not the only fire in hell. The brickyard was a miserable, backbreaking place to work, and if perversion was prevalent in other places, it was an epidemic here. The empty kilns, the tunnels, and the crusher house were tailor-made for the homosexual and for the moonshiner. Some of the best prison whiskey I ever tasted was made in this area, which was outside the main walls, just north of the old criminally insane ward.

Work began there at seven-thirty each morning. At 11:45 the crew prepared to go to dinner. They returned at one and worked until 4:00 P.M. This was the schedule each weekday, and the only way a man could get any respite from this toil was to come up with something that would impress the doctor, and this was not an easy thing to do.

I worked on the off-bear* in 1927 with a fellow named Frankie Brennan, alias Frank Delmar. He was an old hand at

---

* Taking bricks from a moving belt and stacking them on a car for transfer to a kiln.

the job and helped me considerably when I first started, and I soon became adept at the rather tricky work. One day Frank was sick, and I had a new helper. At noon we went to the hospital to get some oil for our hands. This fellow decided to try and get out of work by playing sick. He went into the doctor's office, and the doctor said, "What the hell is the matter with you, Slim—if anything?" Slim fidgeted around, shuffled his feet, and spoke in a whining voice.

"I've got 'cranial edema,' doctor."

"You've got *what?*" the doctor fairly screamed.

"Cranial edema—I've always been bothered with it."

The doctor looked as if he would burst a blood vessel and then said, "I never heard of it."

Slim replied quickly, "I never did either, doc. That's why I'm so worried. It sounds awful though, don't it?"

The doctor was speechless for a moment and then said, "Yes, it does, and it's these things we never heard of that are so dangerous. But I've got just what you need." He called an officer and said, "Put this nut in the hole till he feels better."

All day long the men were kept busy wheeling the "shale" and loading the kilns and the box cars. Rain or shine the work went on, and it was a terrible place when the shale got wet and slippery. Very little of the work was done under shelter. A man was put to the acid test here, and those who failed it received no consolation. They were given a diet of bread and water until they were too weak to stand, and then brought back and told to try it again.

The power plant was located inside the walls then, and it, too, was a den of iniquity and a torture house beyond words. The coal was pushed in small cars on a narrow-gauge railroad called the Nickel Plate. The distance was about a quarter mile, and this line was kept busy winter and summer, and it was operated by convict power. Only the very fittest survived this job for long. The coal was dumped behind the plant, and then other men wheeled it into the boiler room in wheelbarrows. The plant used about sixty to seventy tons of coal every twenty-four hours. Each shift had a lead fireman who watched the gauge and signaled when the other firemen should fire up. These men became very adept at rattling the shovel, and each could be identified by his unique sound. The firemen were almost constantly firing the boilers, which were fed from both ends.

The fires were cleaned every hour, and this was a torturous job. A man had to be a fire-eater and a smoke-inhaler to handle it. One fellow told me, "This is the job they give you when they want to get you ready for hell."

It was here that I had my first talk with Fred Bissell, "The Monster from Hell." I had known Fred long before he committed what was perhaps the most heinous crime ever committed in Kansas. I had also known his parents, and fine old people they were. I knew the little girl who became his victim, and her mother. In fact, the girl was attending the same school as I when this tragedy occurred. I had felt hatred and bitterness toward Fred when I first came here, and I vowed I would never speak to him. However, as time went on and I saw how he had suffered, I decided that I had no right to judge or condemn. I wanted to know how he would tell his story, or if he would tell it at all. I knew most of the facts concerning the case, and I was surprised that Fred not only agreed to discuss it with me, but that he did not deny many of the known facts. The thing that amazed me was that the authorities had seen fit to release him from custody in 1912 when he had been convicted of a prison crime against nature. Why did they not recognize his sadistic and perverted tendencies at that time? Even when I was a boy I recognized them from his actions, his speech, his appearance, and his sneaky way of approaching an immoral subject. He was labeled by most of us youngsters who knew him as a dangerous man. But in spite of these telltale marks he was released to commit what was no doubt one of the most vicious crimes ever committed, at least in our time and this area. He was paroled on April 20, 1915, and committed the crime in 1916.

In that year Topeka, Kansas, was a small prairie town of about 45,000 souls who believed that the stories they read about murder and rape were the results of someone's imagination rather than stark reality. These easygoing, religious people did not give any thought to the idea that such a thing could ever happen in Topeka. But it did happen, and it put a stain on the city which will never be fully erased. Even at this late date, many people make the pilgrimage to the Topeka Cemetery on Memorial Day to put flowers on the grave of little Edna Dinsmore.

Fred's parents were very well-liked old people. In fact, they were loved by the school children who attended Lincoln School, near which the old folks operated a small bakery. The mother baked pies and cookies, and the father delivered the wares in a pushcart. Mr. Bissell always managed to save a few cookies for the kids at the school, who always looked for him about recess time in the evening. He was seldom late. The old folks enjoyed this little gesture as much as did the children. Mrs. Bissell always asked him if he had plenty for the kids at school.

Mr. Bissell was a tall, stoop-shouldered man who seldom spoke unless asked a question. When this happened, he was never at a loss for a logical answer. There was no doubt that he really enjoyed visiting with the children and was proud when they waved at him as all did whenever they saw him. It is difficult to believe that such a beast as Fred was their son.

It was early in 1916 when Mrs. Dinsmore, a widow with a nine-year-old daughter was finding the going a bit rough. She became acquainted with Mrs. Bissell, and they reached an agreement whereby Mrs. Dinsmore would help the old lady with the baking and housework in return for board and room for her and the child. This worked out fine for a time, as it was close to school and the two at least had a home. Fred was staying at home then. He was not working, but was running around and bothering all the women—and boys—he could find to molest. It is a mystery how he kept from being detected, but apparently he covered his tracks well. Fred was especially good to the little girl and gave no signs of having any plans for her. She called him Uncle Fred, which was customary in those days for a child addressing an older person who was a close friend to the family. His apparent unconcern about her is what threw everyone off guard. He did, however, make advances to Mrs. Dinsmore and was promptly discouraged. This, according to Fred, was what brought on his crime. He was hurt inwardly at being turned down, and his horrible plan gradually grew into being.

One night Fred heard Edna tell her mother that she needed some new schoolbooks for a class she was about to enter. The mother told her that she would get them for her as soon as she could, but that she didn't have the money at the present time. Fred said it was at this moment that he knew he was going to rape the child. However, he said he had no intentions of murdering her. He lay awake that night, planning how he would do the deed.

Fred left the house early the next morning, and when Edna was about a block from school, he met her. She said, "What are you doing here, Uncle Fred?"

"I was waiting for you," he replied. "I heard you tell your mother last night that you needed some books. I have a friend over on the west side of town that has all kinds of books. If you want to walk over there with me, you can pick out whatever you need."

"But I would miss school," the girl replied.

"That's all right. I'll tell your mother, and she will write you an excuse," Fred told her.

"I guess it will be all right. I do need the books, and Mama will be surprised when I get them myself. Let's go." She was very happy and had no idea that in a few hours she would be dead—brutally mutilated.

When they got to Sixth and Kansas Avenue, Fred told Edna to wait for him. He said he wanted to make a phone call. He went into a drugstore, and although he didn't know it, this was his undoing. When he came back, he had a small package in his pocket. It contained iodine and gauze.

The two walked west on Fifth Street to a large house that sat on a terrace. As they approached the front door the little girl said, "This house looks empty, Uncle Fred."

"My friend lives in the basement," he said. As they got to the door, he placed his hand on Edna's mouth and dragged her inside and down the steps. The story of what happened for the next six or seven hours is too horrible to print. According to his own story, he resorted to every sort of torture he could think of. When this appetite was satiated, he spent the rest of the day assaulting her. He sat and smoked cigarette after cigarette between assaults. He described the cries and groans of the bleeding and dying child. I found it difficult to control myself as I listened, but I wanted to hear it from his own lips.

When he finally decided he had better go, Edna was still alive. He tried to set the house afire, but the fire department arrived before any damage could be done, and it was the firemen who found the dying girl. She died in agony a few minutes after being discovered.

The officers found the remains of the articles Fred had bought that morning, but there were no other clues as to who the killer might be. No one could recall having seen the girl in that vicinity until a mail-carrier happened along on his way home from his route. He did remember seeing her that morning with a man. The sheriff asked him to scan the crowd that had gathered and see if he could spot the man. After looking the crowd over, the mail-carrier pointed to a man and said, "That is the man." It was Fred Bissell—he had returned to the scene of his crime. He was arrested and taken in for questioning. In the meantime a mob was forming outside the jail. Fred was questioned until late in the night and was released. It was not until his picture had been recognized by a Mr. Souther, the drug clerk who had sold the articles that morning, that Fred was rearrested, and this time he confessed.

By this time, the mob, led by Phil Billard, a well-known Topeka boy, who owned the fastest car in town and whose father was mayor, was really fired up. The sheriff, Hugh Larimer, realizing that he would have to get this fiend away or lose him to the mob, sneaked him out the back door and sped away toward Lansing. The mob discovered the ruse almost immediately and took off in pursuit, led by young Phil. Near Lawrence, the mob was about to overtake the law car when the sheriff recalled a shortcut. He fooled the mob for a moment—just long enough to allow him to drive in through the west gate at the penitentiary a few feet ahead of the angry citizens. But the danger was not yet over for Fred Bissell. The convicts had heard of the crime and were prepared for him. They had ropes and tar and feathers with which to handle him had not the officials found out and taken measures to thwart them. Fred had to be kept locked alone for several years before he could be allowed on the yard.

According to Fred, and what I have learned elsewhere, he is the only man ever sentenced outside a courtroom. He was sentenced on the highway just inside the Shawnee County limits. There a group of men took an oath to kill Fred Bissell if and when he ever came out of the penitentiary, no matter how long it might be. If any of those men are still alive, and I feel sure there are one or two, this oath would still be in effect. However there is no danger of that happening now. Fred Bissell died in Lansing on March 7, 1950.

The aftermath of this crime is almost as tragic as the original act. Shortly after Fred was sentenced, his mother died. The doctors said she died of a broken heart. The father survived a few months, then he too died of the same cause, according to medical authority. After I had heard Fred's story, I said, "Fred, you know you killed your mother and father just as if you had shot them, don't you."

"Yes," he replied. "I guess I did, and believe it or not, I did not want to kill anyone. I just never could control my sex drive. I surely must have been crazy. I guess I still am."

There seems to be little doubt that Fred acted under compulsion, which is, I believe, an insistent, repetitive, and unwanted urge to perform an act that is contrary to the person's ordinary wishes or standards. Certainly this does not excuse the act, but it causes us to wonder why these traits were not detected sooner, and if they were, why such a man was turned loose to commit such a horrible crime. That he suffered every minute of his life after this crime, there is no doubt. He was hated and despised, even by Tom Ramsey, "the Cat Man," who confessed to a crime about equal to that of Fred Bissell's.

Tom Ramsey was serving a year-and-hang* sentence for the murder of his mother. He confessed to killing her, cutting her into small pieces, and feeding her to the hogs. However, there is much more to this story than appears on the surface.

I suppose I knew Tom better than anyone here, and for some reason he trusted me, perhaps because I was interested in him. This interest was not because I could excuse his act—if he was guilty—but because something about his actions seemed to indicate that he was not telling all the truth about the crime.

To say that he was eccentric is putting it mildly. Most folks said he was outright insane. He was antisocial, and he seemed to be obsessed with the desire to impress people with his guilt. This was the main reason I was skeptical—he tried too hard to press the point. I had always felt that there was something

* The law that allowed a prisoner to be sentenced to serve one year and then be executed.

that he wanted to share with me, but I was not sure until shortly before his death. When the story was finally told, I was not too surprised, but I was amazed to learn that any human being could have such a feeling of loyalty toward another as Tom apparently had for his younger brother.

On Sundays and holidays, Tom could be seen parading up the street dressed in an old claw-hammer coat and a battered plug hat and wearing a green tie tied in such a way that one end hung down below his belt and the other was about to slip through the knot. That hat was his prize possession, and where it came from, no one seemed to know. He was always followed by a herd of cats. It was all right to jeer Tom, but there was trouble in store for anyone who bothered those cats. The old fellow was frail and weighed about 110 with his overcoat on, but he would fight at the drop of a hat in defense of his feline companions.

When it became apparent to Tom, and to almost everyone else, that his stay on earth was about to end, he sent word that he wanted to see me. I sat by his bed, and we talked about first one thing then another. I knew that it would be foolish to press him, but I felt sure that he was going to tell me something before he went. I couldn't be sure what it was, but way down deep I felt that whatever it was, it would justify my belief in his innocence. I had never mentioned this feeling to Tom, and that is why I believe he told me the truth. I asked him how he could justify his regular church attendance with his atheistic beliefs. I discovered that this, too, was make-believe. Tom believed very much in God, but as he put it, "No one would have believed me if I told them I was a Christian—they would have said I was a hypocrite. A man who killed his own mother could not be a Christian."

It was about three o'clock in the afternoon when I noticed that he seemed to be getting weaker. He was very pale and kept looking at me as if he could hardly bring himself to reveal what he had in his mind. He finally said, "I am going to tell you something that I swore I would never tell anyone. I am doing it for two reasons. One is, I know you will believe me and understand. The other is, I don't want to go away carrying this awful load. If it could hurt anyone, I wouldn't tell it; but everyone concerned is now gone." He paused and took a deep breath. I am sure that he realized that he would have to hurry if he was to get the story told. He began speaking again, and it seemed that with every word a new light came into the faded eyes—a sort of contentment.

"I tell you now, before God, I did not kill my mother. I loved her in spite of the fact that she was a rather hard woman. I understood her. She had not had an easy life. My father and younger brother were mean to her. My father was a drunkard, and I did not care for him; but I thought a lot of my brother and tried to make excuses for his actions by telling myself that he would learn to appreciate mother as he grew older." At this point he did a strange thing. I suppose his mind was rambling a bit. He looked at me with a twinkle in his eye and chuckled. He asked weakly, "Do you remember the Christmas when the boys stole the alcohol from the paint shop and got drunk?" I was surprised that he even knew about that at all, for at that time he paid no attention to anything that went on if it didn't concern him. We both laughed, he with no strength and I with no mirth.

Then he continued his story. "I had been working in the field all day, and I kept feeling that something was wrong. I couldn't tell what it was—just a sort of premonition. I was nervous and kept feeling like I should go to the house. However, I thought the feeling would pass, and I kept on working. It was near sundown when I saw my brother running toward the field. He was waving his arms and shouting something, but I couldn't make out what it was. But I knew that my fears had not been unfounded. Something terrible had happened.

"When I had quieted my brother down enough to be coherent, he told me the story. While I suspected nothing at the time, I recalled later that he didn't seem as upset as he would have had me believe. However, it was just a thought, and it vanished as suddenly as it had appeared. It was not until later that I gave it serious thought. He said that he had been in town all day and when he came home he could not find mother. He looked in the bedroom and found blood spattered all over the wall but no sign of mother." He struggled a bit for breath, but soon went on.

"We hurried back to the house, and what I found when we got there was horrible. It looked like a slaughterhouse. I noticed that there were bloodstains on the window sills, and a trail of blood led toward the hog pen in back of the house. Whoever had done this terrible thing had taken mother's body out the back window so as to not be seen from the road, which passed close in front of the house and was fairly well traveled. When I got to the hog pen, I realized what had happened. Someone had killed mother, butchered her, and fed the pieces to the hogs." By now the old man could hardly be heard, but on his face was a light that I had never seen before. He was unloading a heavy burden that he had carried to the shadow of the gallows and now to death in bed. He was cognizant of the urgency and reached for that little "extra" that some men have, and continued.

"I didn't call the sheriff right away. I wanted time to think things out. The more I talked to my brother, the more I was convinced that he knew more than he had told. Late that night, I accused him and he confessed. He didn't seem sorry, just afraid that he would be hanged.

"At first I wanted to kill him, but I knew I wouldn't. He had always depended on me, and I couldn't let him down now. Mother was gone. There was nothing I could do to change that. If they took my brother, there would be nothing left for me. I decided to take the blame and hope that my brother would go away and make a man of himself somehow. I called the sheriff and told him I had done the job. He didn't

believe me, and told me so. However, he had no choice but
to arrest me.

"The rest is history. I was sentenced to a 'year and hang.'
As you know, the governor never signed a death warrant under that law, so here I am. I made my brother promise that
he would change. Whether he did or not, I can't say. I never
heard of him again." He looked at me for a moment, then
asked, "You believe me, don't you?" I told him I did, and he
seemed contented. A few hours later the Cat Man was dead.

I have kept my promise not to tell his secret until now. I
would not reveal it now except that it has been so long and I
feel that Tom is deserving of this clarification. Do I believe
Tom's story? Yes, in every respect. His boasting of the crime
was to offset a fear that he had that further investigation
might not be good. He did this so long and so sincerely that
he began to believe it himself.

The incident that he unexpectedly mentioned during his
story was a humorous one that could have been serious except
for a quick-thinking warden. I relate it now simply because
of its value in learning to evaluate people, and also because I
feel that Tom would want me to do it. It was one of the few
things I ever heard him chuckle over.

The old paint shop was located in the west end of the same
building as the power plant, or rather, connected with it. The
shop had just received a shipment of a fifty-gallon drum of
denatured alcohol. This was before the authorities learned
that some prisoners will drink almost anything that smells
like it might have some alcoholic content. Two days before
Christmas a gang of hoodlums stole the drum and hid it somewhere. Due to the excitement of the coming holiday and the
fact that the shop was not working, it was not missed until
Christmas Eve, when the men began showing up on the yard
a little more than slightly inebriated. It wasn't long before
this glow became a flame, and the guards began making ar-
rests. This was not helping the situation, as the men were in

a condition and a mood for almost anything and did not think the guards should interfere in their fun. Just when things were about to get rough, the warden showed up on the yard and told the guards to ignore the men unless things got out of hand. He explained that there was little that could be done now without inciting a riot. "Just stick around and see that there are no fights, and see if you can find out where they are getting their snake juice. I'll take care of them when they sober up."

That was a day of days. Some men were stretched out in the yard, some propped up against buildings or trees, and others had been carried to their cells. Everyone was too happy to fight. They just jabbered, told lies, and had a big time. When it was time to go in, there was no disturbance. Everyone obeyed; of course a few had to be steered and helped, but they made it.

If you have never heard a bunch of drunks talking, you can't imagine the silly things that happened that night. Two men on different tiers were loudly discussing army life. Suddenly, a fuzzy voice came from still further away shouting, "Oh, yeah! Well what about Jess Willard knocking out Jack Johnson? He was pretty good, too." Another yelled, "Hey, Pete, I got a letter from my lawyer tonight. He said for me not to worry. We got 'em right where they want me."

Along in the wee hours things quieted down, and it became very still. I was about to doze when someone belched real loud. That same fuzzy voice piped up and said, "Yeah? Well, you can go to hell, too. I don't have to shut up, and furthermore, you better look out who you're getting smart with; you don't know it, but you're messing with a damn fool." This brought the house down, and there was no more sleep that night.

Next morning, we had almost finished breakfast when the warden came in, strutting and swinging his big cane. He seemed to be in fine form, but not too happy. When everyone had finished eating, he stood in front and began his speech, which was expected.

He began, "Good morning, men. I presume you all slept well last night. However, if you did, I suggest that you do something about your tendencies to curse and shout in your sleep. You did plenty of it—in fact, you did more than plenty." He paused and paraded up and down in front of the tables. He seemed to be trying to make up his mind about what to do. When he spoke again, his voice was soft, almost tender.

"This is the season when we like to make it as pleasant as possible for you men. We have a nice turkey dinner with all the trimmings. This was to have been the best dinner ever served here. It is a shame that you won't get to enjoy it." He waited to let it sink in, then went on, "You had your fun yesterday. Now it's my turn. I don't think you will deny me that right. So—that will be your punishment. No dinner today." He started away, then turned and added, "And you could at least return that fifty-gallon drum—or some of you are likely to miss a lot of meals."

That was the longest Christmas morning—or any morning, for that matter—that we had ever had to endure. Hardly anyone felt like talking. We were in low spirits. As the time drew near when the dinner bell would ordinarily ring, there was no joy in Stoneville. Someone said, "What a heel that guy is, taking our Christmas dinner. He has a heart like a tombstone." Others looked at it more philosophically. They said, "So what? If you dance, you have to pay the piper. I had my fun, and I'm too sick to eat anyhow." The zero hour came and went. No bell. The die-hards said, "I guess he wasn't kidding." We just sat and hoped for a miracle.

About fifteen minutes after the regular dinner hour, the doors were opened and the guards shouted, "All out. Hurry up. Move fast. We ain't got all day to fool around." We wondered what other punishment was coming. It never entered our thick skulls that this could mean anything good for us. They herded us toward the mess hall, but when we got inside the tables were bare. We sat and waited as the guards roamed up and down. Then the captain rang a bell and the waiters came in carrying trays of food—turkey, pie, cake, and all that goes with a good dinner. I heard fellows saying, "I knew good old Ox-tail Bill wouldn't do that to us." Before the bell to begin eating was sounded, the captain held up his hand and said, "The warden wants to wish you a Merry Christmas—and he wants you to dig up that empty drum. He also said that when he finds out who stole that alcohol, it will be rough on them." The drum was never found.

I am sure that the warden who was here at that time is no longer living, but if he is, I am also sure that he would be interested in knowing what became of that steel drum. Well, I am finally going to sing after all these years. The drum was rolled down the alley to the old warehouse that once stood there. The contents were transferred to bottles, jugs, cans, and other containers that had been planted there before. The drum was then taken to the machine shop nearby and hastily cut into small pieces with a torch. The pieces were put in cans of carbide destined for the mine and the cans resealed. When the cans arrived in the mine, the marked cans were opened, the pieces removed, and scattered over the mine in old abandoned entries and gobs.*

These Houdini capers were not infrequent. They were puzzles to officials, but of course to us they were very simple, such as the following incident. One evening just before supper a truck was being unloaded at the kitchen. It had brought a load of sugar in one hundred pound bags. It was found that five of these bags were missing. They could not have been gone more than fifteen minutes when they were missed, but no trace of them could be found. A thorough search was made

* Parts of the diggings that pile up and help support roof of the tunnel.

and a close watch kept for several weeks, but no sugar was found. However, it wasn't too long before there was more whiskey available than was usual, and the price took a slight dip. Here is what happened.

The old icehouse stood just across the street from the kitchen. Some of the more ingenious convicts had remodeled several of the ice-making cases so that they had false bottoms. The sugar was taken there and transferred to those containers, which were then lowered into the floor along with the other ones containing ice. The sugar was kept there for a few weeks, and then the miners began carrying it down in specially made belts of canvas which they could fasten around their waists without showing a bulge. When the sugar was all down, it was distributed to the moonshiners, and—well, the rest is obvious.

It wasn't long after this that old "Cap" Johnny Nicholson caught me red-handed—or red-faced—with a bucket of "hooch." In his nearly twenty-five years of service, he considered this his most clever detective job. He had a hunch that I was up to something—I usually was. I had gone into the division with a trip of empty cars, and on the way out, I picked up a wooden lard bucket full of the happy juice. I had it sitting in the front end of my lead car. I was riding along slowly, thinking how I would stop at the next switch and have a snort. I looked up, and there stood Cap right in the middle of the track. He tried to look stern—you know, like a cop does —but it was a flop. He said, "Aha—I finally caught you. I got you with the goods. You thought you could fool old Cap, eh. All right, where's the stuff—as if I don't know. Come on, and bring the evidence. I'm taking you to the deputy. Now, maybe he will see that old eagle eye ain't sleeping on the job."

I carried that bucket about two miles to the cage. Johnny was walking ahead, and about every hundred yards, I would sneak a little drink. When we got to the top I was pretty well loaded.

We walked into the deputy's office. He looked up and said, "What have you got there?"

"It's liquor, that's what it is. I caught this rascal with the goods." Johnny was puffed up like a pouter pigeon. "I been working on this case a long time, deputy. I knew he was up to no good."

The deputy looked at me, then said to Johnny, "That's shrewd reasoning, John. Hell, I've known that for a long time." He turned to me. "What's that made of?"

"I don't know." I replied. "I didn't make it." He got up and dipped up a cupful and tasted it. "Uh-huh. Not bad." He turned to Cap and asked, "Was he drunk when you arrested him?"

"No, I was too fast for him. He didn't get a chance."

"Maybe so," he said, "but he was too fast for you somewhere, he's drunk as hell now. Get on out of here and take that stuff with you. I'll see you later."

I picked up the bucket, and we started back to the mine. When we got to the bottom, Johnny said, "Go on back to work. The deputy will call when he wants you." I walked off, still carrying the bucket of hooch. I only got about a block away, when I heard old Johnny calling my name and I saw him running up the track. "Gimme that liquor. What do you think you're doing. Gonna sneak off with it, huh." He looked at me sheepishly and then said, "Hell, I forgot to make you dump it out." He waited a moment, then said, "You ain't gonna tell the deputy that, are you? I wasn't gonna let him put you in the hole. You and me are all right."

"Well," I said, "I didn't notice you pleading my case up there." I knew I had him on a limb, and I said, "I'm willing to forget the whole thing if you are."

The last time I saw Cap Johnny was many years ago on a Sunday morning. He was a devout Catholic, and it was his job to come in on Sunday morning and unlock the men who wished to attend mass. My cellmate was a Catholic, and when

Johnny started to unlock the door, he said, "I don't feel so well this morning, Cap. I don't believe I'll go to mass." Johnny stepped back against the railing, put his hands on his hips, and said, disgustedly, "All right, if you don't want to go to mass, you can just go to hell."

Johnny has been gone many years, but I am sure that most of the men who knew him remember him with affection and often recall his humorous remarks.

A new warden came in about this time and decided to loosen things up a bit. He authorized gambling—even built a casino in the bottom of a cellhouse. This was known as Monte Carlo. You could get a game for matches or a hundred dollars, whichever you had the most of. The mine distilleries were working in shifts, and the dope-pushers were doing a land-office business. The warden built a small restaurant on the yard. You could send out in the evening and get a sandwich and coffee if you had the wherewithal. You could get bacon and eggs, toast, potatoes, and coffee for thirty cents. Things were really looking up for us old cons, but it wasn't long before the convicts themselves destroyed the setup as they do so many privileges given them. They stole the restaurant blind, and the gambling casino was the target for a lifer who thought he saw a chance of helping himself get clemency. His caper ended the picnic for once and for all.

It is no secret that almost every time a prisoner is given a privilege, he ruins it himself. There are always the one or two who cannot resist the temptation. Then after it is gone, it is those same ones who holler the loudest that they are being mistreated.

The man who was responsible for the closing of the casino was a man who had been more or less a troublemaker for years. He spared no effort—or no one—in trying to get out of prison. This is understandable, but even in this endeavor there are ethics that most convicts observe.

This man was a first-class mechanic and a shrewd operator

in all his dealings. He thought he saw a chance to help his cause by exposing the gambling—or pampering—activities to the public, and especially to the opposing political party. The penitentiary at that time was an absolute political monarchy, and this man thought that the opposing party would be willing to trade clemency for propaganda that might hurt their political opponents, if not help their own cause. However, even as putrid as politics were at that time, it is doubtful if this material would have been used in the upcoming gubernatorial campaign. It is more doubtful that it would have helped this man, if they had used his evidence. He was a lifer and had a bad record.

His first move was to bribe someone to bring in parts of a camera. After he had all the material he needed, he assembled it and was in business. He had made arrangements for an employee to take the negatives outside for development, and to mail them to the proper persons. He managed to get a few good shots before being observed by an alert guard, who confiscated the camera and the film. This was the beginning of the end for our "happy days." The culprit was kept in solitary for a long time. When he was released and went back to work in the machine shop, he engaged in another caper that about wound up his career. He was caught just after finishing a fine job of building a rifle which was to have been used in an attempt to break out.

Such things as this caused more trouble for the prisoners than they did for the officials. However, it is doubtful if the younger men felt this way about it. Most of them looked upon this man as a real-gone guy, a hero, so to speak. Yet, all he had done was to destroy some privileges that the convicts had been hoping for since the beginning of prisons.

The privileges were not given in an effort to make the convict happy or to detract from his punishment in any way. They were granted, as all good things were then, for a purely selfish reason. The officials were concerned with keeping down trouble, with keeping the men occupied at something pleasing to them so that they would not be so apt to let their minds dwell on malicious things. It worked well. Just how well it worked became apparent as a result of the things that happened after it was discontinued.

Living conditions still had not changed for the better to any noticeable degree. In 1927 a new cellhouse was built, and this relieved somewhat the crowded situation. However, the old cellhouses were just as filthy and gloomy as they had been for sixty years or more. The bugs ran wild, and the rats were just as vicious and hungry. The food was little better than before, except that it was a bit cleaner and was served with a trifle more care. It still had the sickening odor and appeared to have been used before. The fact that there was more freedom of the yard was really a backward step at that time, due to the lack of supervision. There were more knifings, and much less chance of ever finding out who was guilty. This also allowed more opportunity for homosexual activities, which were mostly responsible for the killings.

It was permissible to have curtains across the front of the cell, and no one—but no one—opened those curtains without first making his presence known. To do this was grounds for drastic and sometimes fatal action. The cells could be lit up with bulbs of various colors—plenty of red ones—and some cells had carpets of the finest material from wall to wall. It was not unusual during one of the periodical shakedowns to find women's apparel and cosmetics in many of the cells. In fact, they resembled small boudoirs.

Morphine could be bought at a nominal price from any one of a hundred pushers. If you approached one man and he didn't have it, he could tell you where you could get it. These bindles* contained one or two small pieces of sulphate and sold ordinarily for $1.50. Whiskey—and good whiskey at that

---

* Small packets of dope.

—could be purchased for $1.00 to $2.00, depending on the quality. And the bootleggers used all kinds of attractions to win customers, usually "girls." A man's life could be bought or sold for a few dollars or for the favors of one of the hustlers who infested the yard. These boy prostitutes would "trick" anyone, anytime and any place if the price was right. This was not considered too far out of line. In fact, many of the officials thought it was cute to see one of these characters swishing about the yard making like Fanny Hill.

7

---◆◆◆◆---

Sexual Perversion
in the Prison

For we did not meet in the holy night,
But in the shameful day.

IN THE days of which I now write, perversion was the rule and
not the exception. It was not only tolerated, in many cases it
was encouraged, not necessarily because the officials wanted it
that way, but because they were frustrated. They had no idea
of how to cope with it. The feeling seemed to be, "If you
can't beat 'em, join 'em."

It seems that most people abhor the thought of such happenings, but very few can tell why they feel this way about
them. The fact is, most of us know so little about the real
thing that we listen to others who know as little as we do. But
anyone who has firsthand acquaintance with perversion knows
that it is impossible to use the same yardstick to measure all
cases. Without firsthand experience of associating with and
talking to the people who practice it, there is no way to get
anywhere near the truth.

One physician, in describing homosexuality, has said that
most human beings are labile, varietists, and flexible in their
sexual interests and that their sexual desires and potential
cover a large range. People who are healthy and reasonably
normal take in a large part of this range at some time, but the

pervert restricts his range of sexual activity and only tastes a small part of the real pleasure and satisfaction that the normal person does. It is unfortunate that in our anti-sexual society many perversions are legally proscribed and severe punishments are often leveled against those who perpetrate them. In almost all of today's civilized world, for example, homosexuals, voyeurs, and necrophiliacs are condemned and persecuted.

The doctor goes on to say that most deviates are chronic avoiders of serious issues. They are usually fairly young when they learn to enjoy a limited and disadvantageous form of sexual behavior, and after they see how self-destructive that behavior is, they refuse to undergo the difficult process of re-educating themselves. Many individuals manage to escape from their neurotic or deviated problems, but the fixed deviate gives up, telling himself that it's no use—that he was born that way—and refuses to change.

If we can believe that perversion follows this voluntary narrowing-down of the sexual desires, then it is not too strange that men who have this narrowing forced upon them by incarceration resort to the same thing. However, I can say from fifty years of association with this type of person that this change need not be permanent. I have seen men who practiced this sort of thing for years in prison and never give it another thought after they left—or at least, not enough to continue the practice. On the other hand, there are those who become even worse after release. It is doubtful whether there are many men who were truly born to be sex deviates.

In the old days it was customary to tell the new arrival—especially if he was young—to get his task by selling his body if he could get it no other way. I personally knew one mine boss who had a "kid" and made no bones about it. It was not uncommon for a boss to walk up on men performing a homosexual act and turn and walk away. He was interested in getting his coal; it made no difference how this was accomplished.

There were cases where boys were forced to submit to perversion. It has happened, but I have found during my many years in prison that those cases were the exceptions rather than the rule. In most cases it was by mutual consent, and for many definite reasons other than a sex urge. In many cases it was the "kid" who made the first move, knowing that in this way he could be sure of protection from the masses and of obtaining the luxuries not furnished by the state. They sometimes felt that it would be better to submit to one man than to be free game for anyone who had a desire. Under the circumstances this was sound reasoning, because once a boy was "made," it soon got around that he had no "man" and he was at the mercy of anyone at any time. As far as anyone being forced at knife point—it happened occasionally. However, there was usually something else behind the deal besides perversion.

I have known men who went through most of their life frustrated and confused, little realizing, or even suspecting, that they were being punished by latent homosexual desires. They were fighting against a subconscious desire to do what the conscious mind would not permit them to do. Once this was understood and the proper treatment administered, it was surprising how their personalities improved. I do not think these cases are common, but they do exist.

There was a boy we will call Billy who worked in the power plant. He was a nice-looking boy, rather effeminate, with blue eyes and blond hair. He was not a genuine homosexual. He was one of those who had decided to take the line of least resistance. He was "married" to a big, brutal, sadistic pervert who enjoyed the popularity of being "daddy." He was very jealous and had been involved in several serious scrapes because of Billy's delight in trifling. Billy knew his man would fight for him, and this was pleasing to him. He would flirt with other men in the hopes that there would be trouble.

A new man came to work at the power plant, and Billy, true

to form, made his play. The fellow was con-wise and ignored him. This infuriated the boy, and he decided to get the man into a jam. He went and told his jocker* that the fellow had propositioned him. This lead to words, then real action. In the fight that ensued, Billy's boy friend was getting the worst of it. He drew a shiv and began cutting the unarmed man. He stabbed him eighteen times, and as he was doing the bloody job, Billy was sitting on a ledge high above, shouting, "Kill him, Daddy! Kill him, Daddy!"

Billy's champion tried his best to do as he was told, but by some act of mercy, the man lived. His assailant went to solitary for about a year and was then paroled. Billy got another man and continued his nefarious practice until he was finally killed by another "kid" over another "man."

The case of Sam and his "wife," Carl, is typical of many such incidents, in that it had such far-reaching effects. Three men died and one wound up in an insane ward, all because of a "girl" who could not resist the temptation to cheat on a man. It is also a good example of how fickle prison friendship can be when homosexuality is involved.

In the outside world when legitimate love affairs go awry, it is as simple as walking off and forgetting about it. Not so in prison, where a man's courage is at stake, and pride, if he possesses such a thing. He cannot let another man take his "doll" without retaliating. To do so would mark him as a square. So, when it happens, there is but one thing to do—kill someone. This, of course, is not sensible, but convicts are not noted for doing sensible and acceptable things. If they were, it is possible that the prisons of the nation would not be overflowing. They usually follow tradition, either as they have heard it is done or as they have witnessed it.

Sam and Carl had been "married" for several years and, according to the way they put it, were "madly in love." If we

---

* One who pursues a passive homosexual.

can properly term any male as beautiful, then that is what Carl was. His physical build and his delicate features would have put many bona-fide females to shame. At times I thought his effeminate actions were genuine, and at other times they appeared to be but expert affectation. However, if the latter was true, then I would have to say that he was a great actor. He never missed a cue.

Trouble began to take form when a fellow called "Doo-daddle" came to town. He was big, strong, and handsome and had a reputation for being a first-class hustler and con man, a wheeler and dealer par excellence. He and Carl soon decided that they would make a good team—that is, if they could get Sam behind the proverbial eightball. They knew that this would take some doing, as Sam was no one's patsy.

Both Carl and his new "love" were afraid of Sam—and justifiably so. He had killed at least three men and one woman. They agreed that if they were to be able to enjoy their new-found love, they would have to do Sam in. In fact, Carl told Doo-daddle that unless he killed Sam, they would have to forget the whole thing. The gullible Doo-daddle fell for the line and told Carl he would get Sam the first chance he got.

Things might have gone well for the two plotters except for the fact that some people just cannot "give up the old love for the new." Carl was this kind. He not only went back to Sam, but he told him what Doo-daddle intended doing. However, the hapless chump was kept in the dark as to what had happened, and he still intended to kill Sam. It happened that Sam was not as trusting as the "brat" thought he was, and he began doing a little detective work on his own. He discovered that Carl had instigated the whole deal and that he was no longer trustworthy. Sam was a man of action once he knew what direction he wanted to go. He knew now.

One evening just before the termination of evening yard, we heard loud screams coming from behind a cellhouse. Guards and cons ran to the spot and found Carl lying in a pool of blood. He had been stabbed ten times in the back. Nearby stood Sam, holding a 12-inch shank. The boy was rushed to the hospital nearby, but it was too late. He was D.O.A.

For this caper, Sam was held in isolation for a couple of years and then returned to the population. He looked Doo-daddle up and told him he was willing to let bygones be by-gones. They shook hands and parted. Normally this would have ended the deal. But prison is not usually that way. The older prisoners felt sure that this was not the end, and they were right. Another chapter took place two evenings later.

Sam walked out to the baseball ground the next evening and saw that Doo-daddle was playing baseball. He had his shirt off, and Sam could see that he carried no weapon. Sam waited until the unsuspecting man came in to bat. When he stooped to pick up a bat, Sam moved before anyone could stop him and stabbed the helpless man to death. Sam told the guards, "He stole the only woman I ever loved." The cycle had moved one more turn. And the end was not yet.

There was a walled-in yard behind the isolation cellhouse, with cells where men were locked up to break rock during the day. It was customary to have two men in each cell. Sam was put in a cell with Jake Hightower, a killer from Topeka who had killed another convict shortly before. Jake protested this, saying, "I don't want that man in my cell. It won't work. One of us will be killed." However, his protests were ignored.

The first day went all right, and again that night Jake asked boss not to put Sam in with him again. But the next morning they were together again. About ten o'clock that morning, Sam made a fatal mistake. He stooped to pick up a rock. Jake hit him on the top of the head with a twenty-five-pound sledge. Although Sam's brains were running down his cheeks, the blow only knocked him to his knees. Jake had to hit him again before he got him down. Sam became number three in the cycle. Jake became number four when he died in the hospital a few years later.

If the foregoing has failed to emphasize what sexual perversion was in those days, here is another one that may do the job. It concerns what I had once known as two very fine men —men with pride, hopes, and principles, but who became ensnared in the choking web of unnatural love and died horrible deaths.

"Ace" was a lifer who was well liked by guards and cons alike. He had always stood for everything that was clean and honest, that is, until he met Jimmy, who also had great promise. Then both fell into the fire of homosexuality, and two lives were ruined and ended. At first it is doubtful if either of these two looked upon their association as a love affair. It was just good, clean friendship. But in time it became tainted, and there was no doubt in anyone's mind what had happened —they had gone the way of almost all flesh.

It was a perfect match for several years. Ace gave the boy everything that money could buy in prison. Then Jimmy, like many others of his kind, found another love. He told Ace that he was quitting him, and the older man said, "O.K., if that's the way you want it, Jimmy, good luck." This should have been enough; but fear is a terrible taskmaster, and Jimmy and his new friend decided that they would have to kill Ace before he got them. They convinced themselves of this, and it was Jimmy's downfall.

One evening as Ace left the store line with an armload of merchandise, he looked up to see his erstwhile kid standing in front of him with a big knife in his hand. He stopped and asked Jimmy what the trouble was. The boy said, "I'm going to kill you, Ace."

"For what?" Ace asked, as he tried to think what to do. He had no weapon himself, and he had no doubt the boy was serious.

As Jimmy moved toward him, Ace suddenly dropped the

groceries and lashed out with his right hand. The blow caught Jimmy on the jaw, and he dropped like a pole-axed steer. The knife flew through the air and fell several feet away. Ace picked it up, stooped over the fallen boy, and said, "You shouldn't have turned that knife loose." He stabbed the boy in the heart, killing him instantly.

Ace was never tried for the murder. He was already serving a life sentence, and anyhow the authorities were well convinced that he acted in self-defense. He was kept in isolation for a long time and then went back to work in the mine. He was only back a short time when coal fell on him and mashed him badly. He lay in the hospital for a few weeks and died in agony. Shortly after his death it was said that his sentence was to have been commuted to "time served" very soon had he not killed Jimmy. Another unnatural love affair had cost three lives—three because a few months later some of Ace's friends killed the man who had rigged the first deal.

In those days almost every cell was a love nest, a dope den, or both. All but the most important jobs were neglected in favor of these affairs. No one was immune from their aftermath, and while some men were falsely accused of indulging in them, it is likely that most were involved in some way. I have seen these sex acts take place on the yard during a baseball game, in the chapel when one of the rare shows was in progress, and even during church services. Although I have never seen them, I wouldn't bet a plugged nickel that they haven't taken place in the mess hall during a meal. They were that widespread, and so little effort was made to curtail them.

We know that homosexuality exists in prison. It always has, and it always will as long as human beings are kept in them. However, for those of us who knew it at its very worst, the improvements have been very noticeable. These improvements are mostly due to the more stringent requirements for personnel and the sincere desire to rehabilitate men rather than to allow them to stumble through their sentences and return to society in a worse mental state than they were before they came.

In order to better understand the difficulties with which the officials are confronted in combatting this practice, it is necessary to know more about the different types of perverts with which they must cope. Some people ask, "Why not just isolate them and forget about them?" That is a good question, and it would be a good plan—IF. If it was possible to tell who is who. If it were possible to put a guard with every man every hour of every day and night—which it is not—it MIGHT stop part of it, but not all. If a guard was placed on every tier and ran back and forth as fast as he could; but if he happened to stumble, the deed would more than likely be done before he could straighten up and begin running again.

The bona-fide homosexual is known as a Queen and is a woman in every respect except that the sexual organs are those of a male. This type possesses all the characteristics of a female, and in most cases can don female attire and fool even the experts. They are almost always jealous of true females and have no use for them. Their every action is feminine; they move the funiture about and worry about the curtains and such trivia. They are heavy users of perfumes, and no matter where they may be, they seem always to have cosmetics.

These not only enjoy the actual consummation of intercourse, but like to be led up to the point in the same way as a female, that is, being fondled and caressed. Most of them claim that they cannot be thrilled except by a man. This is probably true, because their desires lean only in this way. They have convinced themselves that they are women, and they believe it.

Another type is the "manufactured" type. These are in no way under compulsion—and do not claim to be—they act for the profit or protection that they feel they need and can get in this way. Some of these are victims of a morbid curiosity that wound up getting them into something that is easier to get into than it is to get out of. This type is commonly called "punk," "brat," "gazooney," "singer," and "dancer." This type is less desirable than a true Queen and cannot compete with one with any degree of success. These are the more pitiful cases. They are usually confused and frustrated all through life. On the other hand, the Queen is happy, because "she" is living the only sexual life she knows—or wants to know. She feels no shame, and if it were possible for her to make any changes, the only one she would make would be to change complete—physically.

It should be remembered that homosexuality takes many forms. There are those who practice sodomy, and others who practice oral copulation. Either of these are apt to engage in off-beat perversions of various kinds, which we cannot describe in print, but which can be imagined by the more active and understanding minds. It is doubtful that many of these— if any—are what could be called naturals. They are more than likely prompted by a self-imposed compulsion, or from plain orneriness and desire for a new thrill. The latter type are more common on the streets than in prison, for in prison, regardless of what a man may think of himself, he must consider, to a point, what the other prisoners think of him. This feeling is not prompted by shame, but it is just good politics.

It is common in stir for a man to brand another one queer if for some reason he doesn't like him. Others pick this up, and without making any effort to find out if it is true, accept it and spread it around. I have known men who became branded as homos and didn't even know they had the beef. These stories gain momentum, and before long it is a foregone conclusion that so-and-so is "geared," and this sticks to the innocent man.

Like crime, I do not believe there is any way that we can force people to refrain from the practice of homosexuality. They must be made to *want* to refrain from it and its character-staining effects. Proper religious instruction—not fanaticism—and the providing of clean, exciting places of recreation can be a big factor in the battle against sexual abuse. Something must be offered whereby people, especially young people, can find something they can place above such activity. But regardless of what is done, the proper place to begin is in our free society. If headway is made there, then less perverts would be sent into prisons to make the task more difficult than it is.

The homosexual is not, as many people think, always a pantywaist or cream puff. Some of the toughest men I have ever known had homosexual tendencies in one way or another. If I were to mention the names of some of these men —which I will not— it would be a surprise to a good many citizens throughout the nation, because many of these criminals have been highly publicized in years gone by.

When you hear or read about the laxity of prison officials in permitting this practice to continue, remember, they are not magicians. They are the ones who truly have a mission impossible. It is not being condoned. They are fighting it in every conceivable way. If society will fight half as hard to erase it from its ranks, the prison officials may someday be able to say, "We have it partly under control." But they will never be able to say truthfully, "There is no homosexuality in our prison." This will never be possible.

I knew a man who had been elected High Sheriff of a county in another state. He was convicted of committing homosexual acts with juvenile prisoners. I talked with this man and what he told me is worth repeating. He said, "I started out with the sincere intentions of helping these boys to see the error of their ways, and somehow I wound up entangled in the same web I was trying to get them out of. I never understood before this happened that a man can get involved in these things so easily, without even realizing what is happening to him. And once he is caught on the hook, there is little he can do to help himself. I'm not even sure he wants to be helped deep down in his heart." This confession convinced me that temptation and compulsion, whether it is self-imposed or due to mental weakness, respects no one, regardless of station in life or inbred beliefs.

However, all the fights and killings in prison are not caused by perversion. For instance, there is the case of "the Fighting Fool."

His name was Denny O'Reilly. He was about five feet, six inches in height, weighed about one hundred and fifty, and had a thatch of blazing red hair. I would say that he was a champion in his own way. He had at least two hundred fights while he was here, and he never did come close to winning one —and neither did he ever admit that he was beaten. His heart was as big as the universe, and he was a sport from the word go and was well liked by friends and opponents alike. The words hate and grudge were not in his vocabulary.

A deputy warden once asked Denny why he didn't stay away from the fellows who were always fighting with him. He replied, "Stay away from me friends? These men are foine gintlemen and real good sports. Why, dippity, if a man can't have a brawl wid his friends once in a while, there'd be no point in livin'."

Occasionally the fellows would get together and arrange for one to start a brawl with Denny. They liked to see him go at it, knowing there would be no serious harm done. Denny despised anyone who would use a weapon—or as he called it, weepon. He was strictly on the up and up, and was noticed several times laughing while absorbing a first-class whipping. He loved to fight and considered it a sport, not an act of hatred. Only once did I see him as much as knock a man down, and this was a dive just to give the little gamecock a boost in morale. He went around for days after this, flexing his muscles and asking everyone, "Did ye see me Sunday punch? I would've kept him down, only me timin' was a bit off."

Many times I have seen the little fellow down, bleeding and

all but out. He would look up at someone with a sickly grin, lift a hand, and say, "Lend me a hand up, pal—me foot slipped." And when he was up, whoever he had been fighting stood clear, because he knew if Denny had an ounce of strength left, he would try to lower the boom.

When it came time for Denny to be discharged, every man he had ever fought who was still here, as well as most everyone else, gathered to wish him well. They presented him with a big card that read; "With admiration and respect for Denny O'Reilly, THE FIGHTING FOOL." As he looked away to keep from being caught with tears in his eyes, he said, "Ye're a foine bunch o' guys."

I wish I could end the story of Denny O'Reilly here, but there is more to it. He went out and married a fine girl, and they had two lovely children. Denny had a good job, and it looked like he had it made—then maybe he had got his "timin'" back. But along came the war, and Denny couldn't resist the thought of a good fight. He enlisted. Knowing Denny, I feel sure that he gave the Japs a good battle—that is, until a sniper's bullet cut him down just before it was time for him to come home. Of course I wasn't there, but it isn't difficult for me to picture Denny as he lay dying, lifting up a hand and saying, "Lend me a hand up, pal—I guess me foot slipped."

Another case which was not charged to sex was the killing of "Peanuts." He was a likeable fellow and always playing. He worked in the dining room with a friend whom he had been close to for many years. They were always together, and as far as I knew, they had never had words before. This was about the time a song was popular called "Three Little Fishes." It happened that Peanuts liked the song and his friend did not. In fact, his friend had a violent dislike for it. Peanuts, being the sort of fellow he was, knew how his friend felt and made it a point to whistle the tune when he was around. The fellow told Peanuts not to do it, and that only encouraged the playful Peanuts. Finally, his friend told him that if he did it again he would kill him.

There was a runway between the dining room and the kitchen at that time, and just inside the door was a pair of Fairbanks scales. There were three or four heavy weights sitting on top of the scales, and as Peanuts came through the door on his way to the dining room, his friend hit him in the head with the one pound weight and knocked him down. Then he leaned over him and stabbed him in the heart with a homemade dagger, fashioned out of a hackle tooth* from the twine plant and a piece of a broom handle. Peanuts was dead when they got him to the hospital.

This was another of those senseless and meaningless killings, and it serves to emphasize the dangers that lurk at all times in every nook and corner of the prison yard. It shows the terrific tension that men are burdened with but that they themselves seldom recognize as being so severe. Such happenings as this are proof that students of psychiatry and psychology could find no better training-ground than the prison yard. It is here that fears and hidden traits come to the fore and the very best and worst in men become evident at the least provocation.

It is fear that is behind most crime. Fear of something—of bodily harm, of want, of losing one's family, even of facing what the average convict thinks is an antagonistic society.

The average prisoner will say that he knew no fear while here. This is probably true in a sense. He did not recognize the restlessness and irritability as fear. It is subconscious and is often mistaken for something else. Prisons are breeding places for mistrust and suspicions. Some are justified, but most are fancied. But no matter how hard a man may fight against it, it comes, somewhat automatically. If someone offers to help, no matter how sincerely, the first thought is, "I

---

* A part from the machine used in making rope.

wonder what this guy's angle is? He wants something or he wouldn't be offering to help me. He is either setting me up for a fall, or he sees a chance to make something for himself."

There is little brotherly love to be found in prison. Most criminals are interested in only one person—their own self. If they can help an old buddy without it costing them anything, they will go along with the program; but when the blue chips are down and it is a choice of helping someone else or benefitting themselves, it is dog eat dog from beginning to end. A jailhouse poet once scratched the following words on the wall of a cell in the old isolation cellhouse: "A friend is a pal who will stick to the end. A friend is hard to find. Many a man will shake your hand, and share your joys in kind. But there are mighty few, this I'm telling you, who will stick when you've gone the route. They'll whine and quit, and lack the grit—to stick when you're down and out." I am not sure, but I think those words were scratched out by Bob "Big Boy" Brady, who played a very prominent part in the following incident.

Memorial Day, May 30, 1933, dawned warm and bright. The prison yard was bathed in golden sunlight, and a southerly wind blew gently across the grandstand, where several convicts were already sunning themselves while waiting for the day's festivities to begin. There was to be a baseball game between two boys' teams from Leavenworth. This was a usual arrangement on holidays, and the men looked forward to it with much interest.

I had been very ill all winter and had just been given permission to go on the yard. Several friends helped me down to the seats, and I had found a place on the extreme north end just above a water fountain which stood there at that time. I looked over to the visitors bench, which was located against the old fire-hall building, and noticed several guards who had come over to see the game. There were also four or five convicts sitting at one end. I knew all these men, and gave it no further thought at the moment.

The game soon got under way, and the manager, "Dutch Meeker," was scampering here and there seeing that everyone was ready. I looked down and saw that the warden had come out and was leaning up against the water fountain. This was to be his last day. He was being replaced by another warden. As he stood there, I noticed Wilbur Underhill, one of the most dangerous men in the prison, come up behind the official. I was surprised—and a bit frightened—when I heard him say, "Don't move, warden. I've got you." I noticed that he had put a wire noose around the warden's neck and held a gun in his back. As he marched the warden around to the front of the fire hall, I noticed Bob "Big Boy" Brady and Ed Davis taking some other guards prisoner over near the fire hall. The teams kept on playing. They did not know yet that anything was wrong. I remember the boy who was pitching at the time. He later became a big-leaguer. His name was Murry Dickson. Suddenly Dutch Meeker realized that a break was in progress, and he herded the kids into a corner at the west end of the fire hall.

Both Harvey Bailey and Ed Davis had a prisoner and headed toward the front. One guard, realizing that he was not too well liked, decided he had better get out of there. He started running up the street toward the front gate. A convict, whose name I will not mention because at this writing he is still in Lansing, chased him down and brought him back. This convict had a straight razor. It proved to be a hard afternoon for that guard.

When the procession was ready, they began marching in perfect double file toward the center tower on the east wall. The officer on duty there was Pete Kley, and he knew what was happening but could do nothing because of the danger to the warden and the other hostages. When they were beneath the tower, Bob Brady stepped out and ordered the helpless guard to throw his weapons and ammunition down. He did so without hesitation. Then the party marched across the outfield toward the southeast corner tower, where there was a barred door into the tower. This was the old bullring. When they came near, the guard fired a shot down in front of the advancing file. I could hear Wilur Underhill shout, "Kill old Sherman. Show them we mean business."

The warden said, "No, don't hurt anybody, boys. I'll take you out."

It was at this time that Harvey Bailey also shouted, "No, don't kill anyone unless we have to." Bailey was a shrewd and resourceful man, but never a killer. He depended on brains and courage. It was very fortunate for all concerned that at least one of the plotters was more interested in freedom than in murder.

When Wilbur Underhill saw that the guard on the tower was going to be no more trouble, he jabbed the gun in the warden's back, and we could hear him say, "Dance a little for the boys, Warden." The warden, being a man of good sense, did just that; and in spite of the seriousness of the situation, the men on the yard laughed loudly—and I might add that I was surprised that the warden presented such a good performance. He was a big man, and it is not likely that he found the job easy.

The procession stopped beneath the tower, and Bailey told the guard to throw the key to the gate down and to throw the bar that reinforced the lock. The guard hesitated a moment, but the warden quickly told him to do what they said. The door was unlocked; and as the men filed in, several young convicts ran down from the yard and joined in. They were Sonny Peyton, Billy Wood, and a boy named Dobson. There was another muscler-in that came down with the main group. His name was Kenneth Conn. I mention him specifically, because later on he and Sonny Peyton met a sudden disaster while attempting a bank robbery.

Billy Wood picked up the rifle the tower guard had thrown down and took it to the wall with him. He kneeled behind a coal box which sat atop the wall. A guard who had come from the front end around the south wall, ran around the corner of the sisal warehouse; and Billy aimed and fired. The bullet cut the lapel of the guard's coat. He turned on the "air" and zoomed around the way he had come. No one saw him again for several days. I won't mention this man's name, because he is still around somewhere. However, at his age, I doubt if he is "zooming" around much any more.

The wildcat* had been screaming for some time now, and the rest of the prison was in confusion. However, from the actions of the men on the wall, who were getting a rope ready for their slide to freedom, no one would have guessed that they were engaged in a dangerous undertaking.

An outside trusty had just backed a car out of the garage for the daughter of one of the officials, when it was spotted by Bob Brady who carried a shotgun. He leveled the gun on the car, told the trusty to let it sit, and ordered him and the girl to get out—and get gone. They needed no second order. As Bob stood watch, the others, including the warden, began sliding down the rope. Bob was the last down. There was one guard left standing on the wall, and he, realizing that he was a sitting duck, lowered himself to the inside of the wall. He was afraid they might see him and shoot him off the wall as a parting gesture. It was the same guard the convict had chased up the street. He was not able to pull himself up after the gang was gone, and an inside trusty had to run and get a ladder to get him down. The men in the grandstand were calling encouragement to him—like "Turn loose. It ain't far down." And "Be careful. Don't break a leg—I hope." But he was saved by the trusty, who did not make any new friends by his act, as far as the convicts were concerned.

---

* Siren.

The original members of the break separated from the musclers-in as soon as they were outside the walls. Bailey, Brady, Davis, Underhill, Clark, and another man, whom I will not name at this time for certain reasons, took the car that was sitting there, and the others had to steal another one. The original gang took the warden and three other personnel with them. But as they passed near the front of the prison, they made one of them get off. In addition to the warden, they kept Laws and Sherman. They headed south toward the Oklahoma line. They were all denizens of the Cookson Hills, and that was their immediate destination.

The word had been broadcast, and the entire state was alerted. The car containing the fugitives and the hostages was under constant surveillance almost all the way to Oklahoma, but nothing could be done because of the danger to the hostages. At one point a highway-patrol car pulled across the road to block the racing car; but when the escapees stopped and prepared to fight, the law car backed off and drove away— no doubt, under orders from headquarters.

That evening about six o'clock the band reached a point about five miles south of Shawnee, Oklahoma. They stopped and unloaded the hostages. After a heated argument, it was decided to release the men unharmed. Once again the cool head of Harvey Bailey prevailed. Underhill wanted to kill the two guards. But it was he who flipped the warden a silver dollar and said, "Shawnee is about five miles down the road— get yourself a cup of coffee, Warden."

This was far from the end of one of the most exciting and colorful breaks in prison history. Hollywood at its best could not have arranged a break with the smoothness and precision exhibited in this one. Much was yet to happen before finis could be written to this episode, including another daring break, bank robberies, murders, and executions.

"Big Boy" Brady, Ed Davis, and Jim Clark were recaptured and returned to Lansing. They were put in the isolation cellhouse and while there, made friends with several young fellows who had won some acclaim as "hard-noses" here in the prison. They also found an old friend by the name of McArthur confined here. It was not long before another escape plan had been worked out. Brady had won the confidence of the day cellhouse guard and talked him into letting him be the floor-man.* This was the initial step in the caper that followed.

One morning when the day man came on duty, Brady promptly took over and locked the man in a cell. He then released the others, and they gathered up all the wood they could find or tear loose from the floor and built a ladder. They then opened a side door and at the precise moment, made a run for the south wall. They scampered up and over the wall. The guards were shooting from both towers, but no one was hit. McArthur was one of the last over, and as he dropped to the ground outside, he broke both ankles. However, he managed to get himself as far as Kansas City, where he was apprehended.

Bob Brady and his band of youngsters eluded the authorities and made it to the vicinity of Paola, Kansas, where they were surrounded in a wheat field. Bob had an old rusty shotgun that he had dug up near the prison. Undoubtedly it had been planted there long before by some friends. It would not shoot, and anyhow he had no shells for it. But he decided to try a bluff.

Bob realized that he was in a tight spot, but he had made up his mind that he was not going back to Lansing—alive. He told his companions, "I am going to raise up and level this shotgun. When I say, 'Come on fellows, let's fight,' you guys move around and make it look like there are more of us. But do not raise up. Got it?" They said they understood, and Bob jumped to his feet, leveling the gun. He spoke the words that

* Man who took care of a floor or tier of cells.

were to be the signal, and everyone of his "pals" jumped up, threw their arms in the air, and surrendered. The police riddled Bob from armpit to hips on the left side. He died almost instantly. I saw pictures of his body later, and it looked as if he had been stitched from armpits down with an oversized needle. He had made the mistake so many have made—he had trusted too many too often. Fear had again reared its ugly head and taken its toll. For it was fear rather than malice that caused these young men to disobey orders and upset the apple cart.

Ed Davis made his way to California, killing at least one police officer on the way. He was given a life sentence in Folsom Prison. He was there but a short while when he and several others attempted a break and killed the warden in the process. Ed and several of his accomplices were executed at San Quentin for this murder. The second most vicious man to participate in the Memorial Day break was dead.

In the meantime, Harvey Bailey had been apprehended on a farm in Texas and convicted of the kidnapping of an oil tycoon by the name of Urschel. He received a life sentence in a federal prison. Jim Clark and one of the youngsters who had elected to go with him instead of Brady were arrested for participation in a bank robbery and went to Alcatraz. Clark was later brought back here and was just recently released.

The only man of importance still at large was the Tri-State Terror, Wilbur Underhill. Before he was caught and subdued there was hell to pay. The F.B.I. and other law-enforcement agencies were very anxious to capture the dangerous Underhill, but they were not having too much success. He knew the Cookson Hills and had many old friends there. He could dart in and out with comparative safety almost at will. It has been reported that while the hunt for him was at its peek, he went into a probate judge's office in his hometown of Shawnee,Oklahoma, and married his childhood sweetheart, in spite of the fact that it was right next door to the sheriff's office. This, if true, lends weight to the theory that the thrill of a challenge is often responsible for men doing the things they do.

The time came, however, when the law, with its array of trained and efficient talent and its unlimited financial resources, found out that the much-wanted man would be at a certain place at a given time. It is likely that this information came from one of Wilbur's "good friends," although this has never been ascertained.

Wilbur and his wife were asleep one night when the law surrounded the house. They called for Wilbur to give up and immediately opened fire from all sides. The wanted man returned the fire, and a short gun battle ensued. Wilbur was hit, but he ran from the house and escaped in the darkness. His freedom was short-lived, however, as the police followed the trail of blood to the rear of a furniture store in Shawnee. They entered and found Wilbur on a bed. He was, as he himself put it, "Shot all to hell."

It has been said that had the law not been so anxious to get him into McAlester, his life might have been saved. He died as the ambulance entered the gates of the Oklahoma penitentiary. He died where he had begun his career so many years before. This was the end of one of this nation's most dangerous men. He had gone out as he had often said he wanted to go—in a blaze of gunfire.

Harvey Bailey was later returned to Lansing and became a changed man. He became active in church affairs and other self-help programs. He was paroled a short time ago, and at the age of eighty he married an old sweetheart. He is an expert cabinetmaker, and he still works at that trade. He is an active Christian and is well thought of in the community where he now lives.

Sonny Peyton and Kenneth Conn later ran into bad trouble when they tried to rob a bank in southwest Kansas. They entered the bank just after it was opened one morning. The cashier had seen them and suspected something. As soon as he got inside, he went to a mezzanine at the rear and hid behind the curtains with a rifle. When the boys made their play, he ordered them to stand. Kenneth Conn grabbed the cashier's wife and held her in front of him. The cashier waited for a chance, then shot over his wife's shoulder, killing Conn. At the same time another employee shot Sonny in the face with a shotgun. He lived, but both his eyes were gone. He was later paroled and apparently made it all right. All the others were soon accounted for, and the end was written to a spectacular prison break.

Sports were becoming more and more tolerated, and along with it came gambling and corruption beyond belief. The fights were fixed, as were the baseball games. The gambling was controlled by a syndicate composed of both guards and convicts. Many dollars were wagered on each event, and sometimes both fighters were paid off, or certain baseball players were bribed. In spite of the seriousness of these happenings, there was an element of humor involved. Imagine, if you can, a baseball game where several men on each side were trying desparately to throw the game. It is a case of seeing who could outfumble whom. Picture two fighters, each one trying to get a chance to take a dive. Watch the frustration on each face as the opponent refuses to take advantage of an opening that a Mack truck could be driven through. Finally, knowing that something has to be done, one rushes in with his face wide open for a punch, and when it doesn't come, he grabs his opponents arm and pulls it toward his face, then flops like a shot quail. Then watch the winner's face. He seems to be saying, "Why, you dirty double-crosser, you beat me to the punch and put me in the middle."

The dope and whiskey racket was also dominated by certain individuals, usually in the employ of some unscrupulous guards whose only concern was to make some extra money to supplement their pitifully small pay. It was possible to have a man killed for a small fee, or if such drastic action was not deemed necessary, then a good sound beating delivered. Seldom was anyone brought to trial for these offenses. It was almost impossible to get evidence or testimony.

No doubt in reading about the characters mentioned in this book, a person wonders whether or not they are real human beings or some special kind of ogre. The average fellow who is serving time is an ordinary person who has permitted his problems to get too big for him to cope with and who, upon finding himself in the penitentiary, succumbs to tensions and fears to which he is exposed. He will act much differently under better circumstances.

Take the case of a fellow we will call Big Jim. He was a fairly well educated man and came from a good family. He had no reason to pull crooked capers to get money, but he had become indoctrinated to the conniving and cunning of the con men in prison until he could not resist a chance to make a fast buck. He received from his "computer" an order that could have very easily cost him his life. He did lose a lot of friends and the respect of nearly everyone who knew him.

Jim worked on a detail that went outside each morning and returned at night. He used to catch rabbits and sell them to the fellows inside. He had several customers who took all he could bring to them—dressed. He was doing a good business, but suddenly the rabbit supply got low. He had an idea that enabled him to keep on bringing in rabbits—even more than before. But someone noticed that there was a difference in the quality of the meat, and they complained to Jim. He assured them that there was nothing wrong with his product. This delayed the blow-off for a time—until an outside trusty came in and spread the word that they were missing their kittens at the farm. This information triggered a hasty investigation, and it was revealed that old Tom Ramsey, the Cat Man, was also missing some kittens. Big Jim was finally pinned down and admitted that he had been skinning the kittens and selling them for rabbits. The fellows had been eating cat meat for months, but one of them said, "So what? It tasted all right to me. What you don't know won't hurt you."

Old Tom was not so easily pacified. He demanded drastic action. He almost started a one-man rebellion. He contacted the warden and everyone else he could think of, and insisted that the "catnapper" be prosecuted. Nothing was ever done, but no one would eat rabbit again unless it came in with the fur still on it. Big Jim couldn't sell a legitimate hot dog from that time on.

This happened just before the death of Jack Beilstein (or Beelstein), the last of the "year and hang" prisoners except Tom. He and Tom seldom saw eye to eye on anything, but when Jack heard of this caper, he sent for Tom, who strangely, went to see him. Jack sympathized by saying, "How could anyone do such a thing as that?" This remark was ironic in view of the crime for which Jack had been condemned.

In the late 1890's Jack worked for a meat-packing company in Kansas City. He was an expert skinner, and this was his downfall. He bet another skinner that he could skin a cow the quickest, and the man beat him. This infuriated Jack, and he killed the man and cut his head off. It was also claimed that he disemboweled the man and stuck the severed head into the cavity.

I recall the first time I saw Jack performing. It was one morning when I was returning from emptying the waste bucket. Jack came around a corner, waving his bucket over his head and shouting, "Let me alone, you yellow-bellied bastard. You're dead and ain't got no business bothering me. Sure, I killed you. Why in the hell don't you stay dead." I don't mind confessing that I stepped aside and was all set to "turn on the fan"* at a moment's notice. I later found out

* Run away very fast.

that this had been going on for a long time and almost everyone else was accustomed to it.

One day at a baseball game I saw Jack get up, grab his leg, and start hobbling away, muttering to himself. Someone asked, "What's wrong with your leg, Jack?"

He said, "That sonofabitch in the air has got a-hold of it and won't turn loose." Several years before he died, Jack punched one of his own eyes out. He said the man in the air told him to do it. He added, "I have to do what he tells me to do."

Apparently Jack was one of those who never learned to live with the ghost of his scarlet stain. He died a frightened and miserable man, still being chased by the man he had so mercilessly murdered, all because he could not concede that someone could beat him doing what he knew he could do so well. He never could face reality again, although he was given several chances to do so. He was granted a Christmas leave one time to visit relatives in Kansas City. He had been gone just about two hours when a guard saw him running toward the front gate. He was fighting the "man in the air" and shouting for them to open the gate so he could get in and be locked up. It seems strange, but the apparition never came to him when he was locked in his cell.

Certainly whatever these men did here that marked them as eccentrics could be explained by the fact that both had lived in the shadow of the gallows for twelve years, from 1895 until 1907, when the law was abolished. At any time during these years they could have been executed at the governor's order. This strain proved a burden too heavy for them to bear well—especially Jack.

As the number of these condemned men began to diminish, the pressure lightened somewhat. However, this took years, and at one time as many as sixty men were waiting execution. Had any governor so chosen, he could have ordered a mass execution, according to information contained in the *Kansas*

Historical Quarterly. It was Governor Hoch who said that he would resign his position, regardless of how high it might be, before he would become involved in hanging a human being.

8

Capital
Punishment?

Three yards of cord, and a sliding board
Are all the gallows' need: . . .

CAPITAL PUNISHMENT has long been an issue that Kansans
would just as soon forget. However, since its admission to
statehood, Kansas has been torn between the moral and religious right of it and has not been concerned enough as to its
worth as a deterrent to the vicious crimes that are punishable
by death.

It would seem that the majority of people do not really
want this form of punishment, but that they have, in some
way, been convinced that it is the only way to curb killings
and rape. If it does serve this purpose, then the argument
would be good. But does it? It seems a bit ridiculous to even
consider the moral or religious aspects. Any persons calling
themselves Christians could not rightfully condone the taking
of a human life under any circumstances. The commandment
"Thou shalt not kill" refers to each of us. The pronoun *thou*
was meant to include every human being. I have not been
able to find one place in the New Testament where any man
is authorized to mete out death. And for the Christian, this
is the law. If we do not accept the New Testament, we cannot
call ourselves Christians.

It is immaterial what I think about capital punishment, to anyone except myself. But if, as the advocates claim, we are not using this method as vengeance, but as a safety measure— a deterrent—then the fairest and most sensible thing to do is to let the statistics speak for themselves.

Many books have been published dealing with the subject. Some of these were written by competent, sincere writers who were more or less qualified to write on the subject. However, many were written by men and women whose only qualifications were hearsay or material taken from faulty, sometimes incomplete records. They seldom offer any statistics to prove or disprove their theory. It is doubtful that any of these writers have been privileged to talk with many condemned men, and certainly not to have known them personally.

In addition to statistics, I offer my opinions which grew from knowing men who were later executed and others who spent many long, weary, frightening days in the shadow of death. Some of these men I knew before they committed their crimes, and I have firsthand knowledge of their offenses as well as their attitudes before and after.

According to newspaper accounts relating to the argument for and against the death penalty in 1935, it would appear that the advocates of the bill were primarily interested in reducing the number of violent crimes, with which the state was beset at that time. Representative Hatch, a Democrat, introduced the bill, saying that it was necessary because of the loss of life in the crime wave that had struck the state, which was terrifying because the law-abiding citizen did not know when the gangster's machine guns might be turned on him. Mr. Hatch did not believe that these professional criminals— as he called them—were men who could ever be rehabilitated. "Once a criminal, always a criminal" was his belief. John A. Scott, another legislator, who was also a minister, upheld the right to kill by saying that it was provided for in Biblical times, not for vengeance, but for the protection and preservation of society. The only thing wrong with all that was said by these two men was that the entire discourse had but one fact—the rest was opinion. The one fact being that a crime wave had struck the state.

Even if these men were right, the crucial question is left unanswered. Does capital punishment deter the criminal from committing vicious crimes?

Before I offer the statistics as I have them, it seems appropriate to give the reader an idea of the confusion that this subject has always caused. I will leave the answer to Mr. Hatch and Mr. Scott, to the more-qualified theologians in regard to the religious and moral aspects.

Let us delve deeper into the different viewpoints of the general public and especially the newspaper gentry. The To-peka *Daily Capital* of January 1, 1935, offered two reasons why such legislation should be enacted. The first being that public indignation had been aroused when an armed band had robbed, tortured, and killed the members of a farm family a few weeks earlier. The criminals were captured, and it was necessary to confine them in a secret place to protect them from an aroused lynch mob. In the opinion of the editorial writer, the sentiment was that those who commit crimes of this nature have forfeited the right to live. The second reason for reestablishment of the death penalty was that the public was dissatisfied with the parole system and that wrongs suffered at the hands of ex-convicts on parole contributed materially to the rising anger that might restore capital punishment in Kansas.

The same paper on January 18, 1935, did an about face and speaking editorially, criticized the bill for taking an overly emotional and simple attitude toward the solution of the crime problem. The editorial stated that the death penalty would not serve as a deterrent and predicted that the law, if enacted, "will not accomplish any purpose and will be a more or less discreditable and backward step for the state. It will open the door to execution of innocent persons which has sometimes happened. Legal processes are not infallible."

Senator Nelson argued that the state would "have to take action to stop this murder that is going on all around us. In the old days we used to hang horse thieves. Now we put them in the penitentiary and that is all there is to it." However, Senator Logan, a former county attorney, argued against passage of the bill, stating that leaders in criminology, psychiatry, and penology were almost unanimously opposed to capital punishment and concluding that it was impossible to show that capital punishment was a deterrent to crime.

During 1963, 8,540 murders were committed in the United States. In 1964, 9,249 murders were committed. These statistics should be considered at least a small point against the effectiveness of capital punishment in deterring crime. The twelve states having the *fewest* murders per 100,000 population were: Connecticut, Iowa, Maine, North Dakota, Oregon, Rhode Island, South Dakota, Vermont, New Hampshire, Minnesota, Utah, and Wisconsin. It is important to note that eight of these twelve states did not have capital punishment.

The ten states which had the most murders, from seven to twelve per 100,000 population, in 1964 were: Alabama, Alaska, Arkansas, Florida, Georgia, Louisiana, Mississippi, North Carolina, South Carolina, and Texas, according to the *Uniform Crime Report, 1964*. Eight of these ten states did have capital punishment. These two sets of statistics favor the abolitionists, as it is direct argument against the claim that capital punishment deters crime.

This controversy is never-ending; however, it seems that the argument against has been gaining some ground in recent years. This is apparent by the fact that many states have already abolished capital punishment and many others are contemplating some action on it. Its opponents claim that it costs more to execute a man than it does to keep him in prison for a fairly long period of time. Whether this is true or false, it seems a bit barbaric to let the cost in dollars and cents enter into any argument where human lives are at stake.

The opponents of capital punishment contend that offenses resulting in capital punishment are frequently committed by persons suffering from mental illness or that they are of an impulsive nature and are not considered acts of the "criminal class." They point out that it is often the bungling amateur and not the hardened criminal who blunders into murder. They say that when the death penalty is removed as a form of punishment, more convictions are possible with fewer delays in legal procedure. Unequal applications of the law, they contend, take place because those executed usually are the poor, the ignorant and the unfortunate. Although about one murder in seven is commited by a woman, only about one woman a year is executed in the United States.

They further claim that conviction of innocent persons may occur and death makes a miscarriage of justice irrevocable. They cite the case of Charles Burnstine in the District of Columbia, who life was spared just moments before his execution was scheduled and who was released two years later when another person admitted the offense.

Recent publicity in Mountain Home, Idaho, involved the alleged confession of Gerald M. Anderson of the Air Force, who allegedly made his confession under duress, only to see the case cleared up by the confession of another man.

"Where a life may be at stake, the trial is highly sensationalized and adversely affects the administration of justice and is bad for the community," Supreme Court Justice Felix Frankfurter commented; and he added that "when life is at hazard in a trial the whole thing almost unwittingly affects the jurors, the bar, the public and the judiciary."

In the words of the Minister of Justice of Belgium, where the last execution took place in 1863 and the murder rate is now extremely low, "We have learned that the best way to teach respect for human life consists of not taking it in the name of the law."

Those in favor of capital punishment ordinarily rely on deterrence as the principal reason for continuing the practice. They contend that in states where a life sentence is the maximum penalty with a stipulated amount of years to be served, a lenient parole board may release a killer too soon. In other states the average time served on a life sentence is twelve to fourteen years. In Kansas a life sentence does not provide for the privilege of parole. The only exception is when clemency is granted by the governor, modifying a life sentence to a definite term in number of years.

Kansas juries in the past have recommended the death penalty in only a small percentage of convictions for first-degree murder. Since the first legal hanging in Kansas in February of 1863, a total of twenty-four persons had been executed under state law up until December, 1965. At that time there were 111 life termers (109 men and 2 women) in the Kansas penal system, including those convicted as habitual criminals.

Today the possibility of executing an innocent person wrongfully convicted of murder is somewhat remote considering the many avenues of legal safeguards available to all condemned prisoners in the state courts on up to the United States Supreme Court. In Kansas, the average length of time between conviction and actual execution for the last five executed prisoners was four years, the lowest two years and ten months, the highest five years.

James V. Bennett, former director of the U.S. Bureau of Prisons has asked, "Who can say that the continued use of capital punishment has not had some effect in keeping the homicide rate down, even though other crimes punishable by lesser penalties, have increased enormously?"

It is interesting to note that two groups of public servants coming into the most intimate contact with the criminal element have divergent views on the subject of capital punishment. Among law-enforcement officers who are daily confronted with the results of criminal activity, and whose duty requires a careful investigation of the gruesome aspects of murder, rape, and other capital offenses—these men are predominantly in favor of legal executions. On the other hand, workers in penal institutions, who come in contact with the criminal as a man after the deed is committed, and view him as another individual—are predominantly in favor of abolishing capital punishment. This becomes accentuated when they are required to confine men in death row or actually perform an execution.

Jehovah commands, "Thou shalt not kill," and Noah declared, "Who sheddeth man's blood, by man shall his blood be shed." One of these is a Holy Commandment. If we can, for any reason, find a legitimate excuse for ignoring that commandment, then it would seem just as right to scrap the other nine and make it legal to steal, covet, bear false witness, and dishonor our parents. It is that simple.

Many crimes are committed which deserve the very worst punishment that can be meted out. But is capital punishment the most severe? I have talked with men who were about to be hanged, and I have witnessed two hangings in my life; and in the cases where the crime could be termed atrocious, I do not believe the prisoners were punished nearly as much by hanging as they would have been if they had been made to live with their consciences for the remainder of their lives—and don't think they are not bothered by conscience. It is a shameful death, to be sure, but upon whom does the shame fall? Certainly shame means nothing to a dead man. The ones who must live with the shame are the innocent ones—the loved ones and friends. And a certain amount of shame is on those who perform the job and must go on living, wondering if they have done a great or little thing. Why should the living have to go on paying for a crime they did not commit, while the guilty person is excused by merciful death?

I have served with many men who were spared the death penalty for some reason, and I have never seen one who did not suffer the bitter pangs of remorse—if not for their crime, for their inner turmoil and the hopelessness of the future. Although most of them tried desperately to hide their true feelings, it showed in their every waking action, and they found sleep—good sound sleep—as elusive as the proverbial pot of gold at the rainbow's end.

According to a report in the *Kansas Historical Quarterly*, the very first Kansas law legalizing the death penalty became known as a "bogue law." It specified death as the punishment for first-degree murder, but failed to specify by what means the penalty was to be carried out. Then, when this was remedied, the hangings became such gala affairs—sort of social gatherings—that the law had to be remodified to specify that all hangings must be "private" affairs, performed inside an enclosure. This happened after the hanging of William Dickson in Leavenworth, Kansas, August 9, 1870. This execution reportedly was a grave travesty of the law's intentions.

Dickson had been released from Lansing, where he had been serving a sentence for horse theft, on March 7, 1870. On March 10, he was arrested for the murder of Jacob Barnett, a Jewish peddler. The victim, who was well liked in the vicinity, had been shot five times and robbed. A watch belonging to Barnett had been found in Dickson's possession, and feelings ran high against him. A large and rather surly crowd was on hand when the accused man was given a preliminary hearing on March 19. There was some talk of lynching, but nothing came of this threat.

The trial took place at the June session of Leavenworth's Criminal Court. It took the jury but fifteen minutes to find the defendant guilty of murder in the first degree. He was sentenced to hang on August 9, 1870.

The report says, "An old gallows (probably left over from 1863) was set up in the 'northwest angle' of the county jail yard. This site did not fulfill the criminal code's 'private enclosure' provision. The Times and Conservative in reporting the affair said, 'Owing to the prominence of the County Jail Yard, the melancholy proceedings were visible from almost all parts of the city, and thousands availed themselves of the opportunity of seeing the law's victim dropped from earth to eternity.'"

According to the newspaper description of the scene on the day of the hanging:

A stranger in Leavenworth might have thought the attraction was a circus rather than a legal hanging.

Long before the appointed hour of noon, the hills and housetops in the vicinity were crowded with people anxious to see the sad spectacle. The jail was besieged by crowds with and without admission passes. [Sheriff McFarland had invited a large number of citizens to attend the hanging.] Not only this, but all over the city people on housetops and eminences looked with glasses or the naked eye to see the suspension of the convicted wretch.

About twelve o'clock the excitement of thousands who failed to get admission was intense. The officers were pressed for passes, and scores of men and children clamored simultaneously for the open sesame to the judicial slaughter. We regret to be compelled to say that over half the vast concourse which viewed the spectacle from outside points was composed of children of both sexes.

The festive air which prevailed at this hanging showed utter disregard for the law by the ones who were sworn to uphold its dignity. It was this attitude that explains why prisoners were subjected to brutality and filth and caused people throughout the nation to regard this prison as the nearest thing to hell, "The Devil's Front Porch."

According to an article by Louise Barry in the *Kansas Historical Quarterly,* the death penalty has been legal in Kansas for first-degree murder for approximately sixty-eight of the ninety-six years since the state was organized. Or, to state it otherwise, it has been legal for all but the twenty-eight years from 1907 to 1935. Execution by hanging was not specified by law until 1858, but since that year it has been the state's prescribed method of execution.

Up to 1907, when capital punishment was abolished, only nine persons had been hanged under state law. All those executions occurred between 1863 and 1870. During the next seventy-three years there were no hangings *under state law*, but since 1944, fifteen men have paid the death penalty under state law. As of April, 1969, two men were awaiting execution.

Nine other persons are known to have been legally hanged in Kansas. Records have been found of three such executions under military jurisdiction during the Civil War period. Three persons were hanged under federal law at Wichita in the late 1880's, and at the U.S. Penitentiary, at Leavenworth, one man was hanged in 1930 and two others in 1938.

Illegal hangings within the state have been more numerous. More than 200 men have been lynched in Kansas. These outside-the-law executions were largely for the crimes of murder and horse-stealing. Although more than half the lynchings occurred in the first fifteen years of Kansas' existence, some ninety persons were illegally hanged in the state between 1870 and 1932.

Legislation relating to capital punishment for murder in the first degree can be summarized as follows: Among the so-called bogue laws passed by the Pro-Slavery legislature of Kansas in 1855 was a statute dealing with crime and criminals. One of its provisions was "Persons convicted of murder in the first degree shall suffer death." Until the Territorial legislature of 1858 passed a "Code of Criminal Procedure" there was no law prescribing a specific method such as hanging as the means of execution.

However, in 1859 the Territorial legislature repealed all the statutes of 1855 and many of the laws enacted in 1858, including the criminal code. In 1859 the legislature proceeded to pass a new crime and criminals act and a new code of criminal procedure. The former provided that "Persons convicted of murder in the first degree shall suffer death"; and the latter contained a section stating, "The punishment of death, prescribed by law, must be inflicted by hanging by the neck, at such a time as the court may adjudge." Also in the criminal code was the provision "Sentence of death shall be executed in some private enclosure, as near to the jail as possible," with a specific statement as to the persons who could attend an execution either by invitation of the sheriff or by request of the prisoner. The hanging of William Griffith in 1863 was, nevertheless, a public affair; and the hanging of William Dickson in 1870 was a travesty of this section of the law.

When Kansas became a state in 1861, the 1859 acts remained in effect, because the Wyandotte Constitution, under which Kansas was admitted to the Union, provided that all laws in force in the Territory at the time of the adoption of the Constitution should remain in force until they expired or were repealed, if they were not inconsistent with the Constitution. They were slightly revised and codified in 1868, but remained essentially unchanged.

Several sections of the code of criminal procedure were amended by the legislature of 1872. The most vital change was the provision "The punishment of death prescribed by the law must be inflicted by hanging by the neck at such time as the governor of the state for the time being may appoint, NOT LESS THAN ONE YEAR FROM THE TIME OF CONVICTION . . . PROVIDED, that no governor shall be compelled to issue any order . . . for the execution of any convict." In effect, this banned capital punishment, for no Kansas governor ever took this responsibility during the thirty-five years this law existed. (This was the "year and hang" law.) In 1907 a law was enacted which did abolish capital punishment for murder. The law said in part, "Persons convicted of murder in the first degree shall be punished by confinement at hard labor in the penitentiary of the state of Kansas for life." This statute remained in effect for twenty-eight years.

The Kansas Historical Society records tell us that in February, 1871, a few months after Dickson's hanging, a bill was introduced in the state legislature by Senator H. C. Whitney "To regulate the infliction of the death penalty and to amend an act to establish a code of criminal procedure." The contents of this bill are not known, since no copy can be found. But it apparently contained the same, or much the same, provisions as the bill which was to become law in 1872. Of the 1871 bill (which was passed by both houses, but was not signed by the governor) the state recorder later wrote, "If we are rightly informed, Governor Harvey is opposed to capital punishment, but he did not like this law [i.e., bill] because it threw all the responsibility on the governor."

Early in June, 1871, in the district court in Topeka, Mrs. Mary Jane Scales and Lewis Ford, both Negroes, were convicted for the murder, on November 17, 1870, of Burnett Scales. They were sentenced to be executed by hanging on August 17, 1871. Preparations for the hanging included the erection of a gallows surrounded by a tight board fence (24 by 28 feet, and 14-feet high) on a vacant lot south of the Shawnee County jail, with a covered passageway leading from the jail.

Said the State Record: "Hanging by the state is a disgrace to civilization and only legalized murder. Every precaution will be taken to make this murder respectable. The fact that already over 250 applications for witnesses have been made, is evidence of a demoralized condition of society." On the night scheduled for the execution, Governor James M. Harvey commuted the sentences of these two murderers to life imprisonment.

The Scales-Ford case is mentioned only because it was probably the nearest Kansas ever came to hanging a woman, and the action of Governor Harvey served to bring the subject of capital punishment again to the forefront of public opinion.

With the rise of Populists to power in the state, the capital-punishment issue was forgotten, and not until 1905 was there a revival of interest in the subject. That December, a statement by Governor E. W. Hoch said, "I would resign my position, however high it might be, before I would be the one to execute a death sentence, whether the condemned person is a man or woman. Why, the hanging of a human being whether it be legalized or not, is a relic of barbarism."

By the last of June, 1906, according to records, the penitentiary's death-sentence population had increased to sixty men. This was the all-time high. Two years later there were fifty-seven and by 1915 only fourteen.

After the 1935 measure was enacted, it was nine years before a criminal was hanged under this law. Albert M. Zakoura—the first to be sentenced—was reprieved and his sentence commuted to life by Governor Walter A. Huxman on September 3, 1937. The second to be sentenced was Fred L. Brady. When on February 8, 1944, Governor Andrew Schoeppel refused clemency to Brady, M .F. Amrine, Warden of the state penitentiary, resigned rather than to take part in a hanging. After many years of penal work, Amrine became opposed to capital punishment, although he had formerly favored it. As it turned out, Brady was not the first victim of the law. A month before he was hanged, Ernest L. Hoefgen was executed (March 10, 1944) for the murder on September 18, 1943, of Bruce Smoll, an eighteen-year-old college student. Brady was hanged on April 15, 1944. His crime was the murder on January 9, 1943, of Joe Williams, at Arkansas City, Kansas, during an attempted holdup. On the same day Clark B. Knox, a Negro, was executed for the murder on August 1, 1943, of Edward Nugent, a Kansas City policeman. Brady was hanged just after 1 A.M., and Knox about six in the evening. In the next six years three more men were executed, bringing the total to fifteen, counting the nine mentioned before, up to 1950. However, since that time, eleven more have paid the penalty at Lansing.

According to an article in *The Prison Mirror,* the official publication of the Minnesota State Prison, the following statistics relate to men who have served comparatively long sentences for murder and have returned successfully to society:

In Connecticut between 1947 and 1960, 60 convicted murderers were released on parole after serving an average of fifteen years in prison. Only seven of these violated. In California during the same period, 342 convicted murderers were released on parole. Only 37 of these violated. In Maryland between 1936 and 1961, 37 prisoners who were serving life for murder were paroled after serving an average of 16 years in prison. Only nine of these violated their parole. In Massachusetts between 1900 and 1958, ten lifers who were convicted of murder were paroled after serving an average of 22 years in the penitentiary. Only two violated, both for "indiscreet behavior." In Ohio, between 1945 and 1960, a total of 169 prisoners serving time for murder were paroled after serving an average of 22 years in prison. Only ten of them were returned to prison as violators, and only two of these for committing a felony. In Michigan, between 1938 and 1959, 164 first-degree killers were released on parole. Only four had to be returned to prison, and only one for committing a felony. In Rhode Island between 1915 and 1958, 19 convicted killers were placed on parole. Only two of them violated.

Out of 801 paroled murderers, only 61 had to be returned to prison as parole violators, and only a small number of those for the commission of another felony. It should also be noted how many years these men served before they were released from prison.

It seems that the main reason that parole laws have been so stringent is that these boards have been prone to consider only a man's past. This has had a tendency to make men develop an attitude of "What's the use of trying to utilize my time in prison to better myself—the parole board never considers this with the same sincerity that it judges the past." If this practice were changed, it is likely that the average convict would cease blaming environment, parents, distasteful experiences in younger life, and the world in general. The past, as someone has said, can only show why we are where we are, and while it can have some bearing on where we intend to go, should not be considered the sum total of a man's personality and ability. It might be well to consider that if challenge is a motivating power in causing crime, it can also be a power in helping men to steer clear of crime.

In view of the many ingenious plans conceived in the minds of men in prison who make their bids for freedom, it becomes apparent that many fertile and agile minds are being lost to a useless and unworthy cause. When these minds can be turned into the proper channels and put to use for good instead of evil—and it can be done—the world will soon find that it is a winner instead of a loser, financially speaking. For example, take the case of a man we will call Joe.

Joe was a lifer. He had been trying to get something done on his case for many years and was ready to concede that if he got anything worthwhile for himself, he would have to come up with a scheme to "beat these people." He realized that it would have to be something unique, because "these people" were not recognized as dumbbells. He came up with several plans and by the process of elimination decided on the one that he felt was different enough—and daring enough—to do the job. He understood that in taking this route he was making himself subject to retaliation by both the officials and the convicts. However, he was not a craven creature, and he did want out. He elected to give it a try. He managed over a period of time to make arrangements to get a couple of guns smuggled in to him. When this was done, he hid the guns in a safe place and literally "forgot about them." He waited nearly two years, then he decided it was time to make his move.

Quietly and shrewdly he got word to the warden that he

had some important information for him. This is always a good ruse, and it worked then. He told the warden that he thought he knew where there were some guns hidden and that he would get them and turn them over, but he must be shown some consideration because his life would be in danger if he had to stay inside the prison. Negotiations got underway, and he was told that he would be granted a parole if he produced the guns as he said he could. Of course he could—it was a dead mortal cinch.

The guns were produced, Joe was branded a fink, but he walked out the gate a free man. It is likely that many men who knew of this caper have always considered Joe a stoolie. However, Joe hurt no one, and the ones who have always wondered who the guns really belonged to, can stop worrying.

Another example of ingenuity is connected with a case I related earlier, but which I discontinued purposely for various reasons—one of them being to avoid any controversy.

When the plot was set up for one of the breaks, the big problem was not how to get guns into the prison, but how to get the money to pay for having the job done. This phase was left to one of the ringleaders, who was very cunning and also very well liked. He invented a dandy scheme, and I doubt if there are five men alive who know the truth, although many took part in the scheme.

In those days it was permissible to take up a collection among the prisoners for any worthy cause, and the men were always very generous in these cases. The ringleader knew this, so he arranged on a visit to have his mother write him a letter telling him that if she didn't get money to pay off a note, she would be evicted from her home. This letter was tacked on the bulletin board, and the do-gooders got busy and began taking up a collection. It easily netted more than was needed for the project. It is doubtful if the outside participants knew what was taking place. However, the mother forwarded the money to where she had been instructed. The guns came in later in a shipment of merchandise. The plan had worked.

So we find that there are supple and active minds in prison, just as there are suspicious and unscrupulous ones. It is easy to find a fierce loyalty on the one hand and a complete disregard for principles or friendships on the other. The two following stories are good examples of the fruits of misplaced trust and friendship. They also show how low a man will allow himself to fall when he permits imprisonment to take over his entire soul, his self-respect, and his pride, when he will sell the life of a friend for nothing more than a pat on the back and perhaps a few extra months of freedom.

Roger Coe was a nice-looking young man, well liked, well educated, and well on his way to defeating the environmental factors and the misguided attitude that caused him to commit robbery and receive a prison sentence. It was almost certain that before too long, Roger would be paroled. He was a well-behaved boy and was thought much of by the entire prison population and the personnel. He had many letters from the community in which he had been born and raised, recommending that he be given another chance at the earliest possible time. However, he made a mistake that so many of the younger men make—he allowed himself to idolize a man who, according to his own story, was a late edition of Jessie James and all the other criminal celebrities combined. This fellow had a fast tongue and a way of selling a bill of goods. It seems that this always captures the fancy of young men.

Roger swallowed the tales told him by this self-styled Jimmy Valentine, who, according to his own admission, had taught Pretty Boy Floyd and Al Capone all they knew about crime, and who in reality had never shot anyone—except himself, with a hypodermic needle.

Roger worked at the power plant, which had been moved from inside the walls and was enclosed by a high wire fence. He became acquainted with another young fellow who had already built up quite a reputation as a bad man and who, unlike the older friend, had credentials proving his courage and exploiting his criminal tendencies. As time went on, Roger divided his time between the two acquaintances. He kept the fact that he and the younger man were planning an escape from the other friend for a long time, but at last, unbeknown to his plotting partner, he unfolded the plan to the older man, whom we will hereafter refer to as John. He held back no detail—possibly hoping he could get some helpful information and encouragement from John.

The two boys made their bid as planned. The light switch was thrown off, pitching the prison into darkness for a few moments. They scaled the fence and began to run for the safety of the brush and buildings about a hundred yards away. But when they hit the ground, the lights came back on, much sooner than they had planned, and the tower guards began shooting. Roger's friend, who was more experienced, made it to safety, but as he looked back, he saw that Roger was down. He could have gone on and perhaps made his escape, but he was not that type. He turned and ran back into the blistering fire, hoping he could rescue his pal. As he reached Roger a bullet hit him in the thigh, and he was helpless. They were both taken to the prison hospital.

The doctor said that Roger could live only a few hours, but that his buddy would be all right in a few weeks.

The next morning I accompanied the chaplain to the hospital to see Roger. He was conscious and fully realized his predicament. It was while I was there that John, the boy's idol, came in. He blubbered and tried in every way to show his great grief, but somehow, even then, I couldn't buy the act. He vowed his great friendship and told Roger that when he was released from prison, he would go personally and see his mother. Roger died a few minutes later, and perhaps it was my imagination, but I thought he looked at John as if he suspected the truth.

That same day the word got around, as it has a habit of doing in prison, that the boys had been set up; and it wasn't long before it was a fairly safe bet who had done the setting. Just a few minutes before the other convicts were to hold court on the traitor, he was whisked out the front gate and was never heard of again as far as I know. Yes, it was Roger's hero, the man he trusted, who sold him down the river for a few months of extra freedom. But is he free? One can only wonder whether he sleeps well at night, if he is still alive. This is an example of the so-called honor among thieves, which seldom exists. It is a taste of the bitterness and unfaithfulness that finds its way into the hearts of men after long years of drudgery and routine. It is proof that there is no limit to the depths to which a man can, and often does, fall, when he finally discovers that "If you dance, you must pay the piper."

No doubt many will wonder why if the authorities knew of the plan, they did not just prevent it from happening. To anyone who is familiar with prison administration, the answer is simple. The authorities had only a convict's word. They could not be sure that the information was correct. If they accepted it as true and put the alleged plotters in the hole, they would have never known for sure and would have been obliged to release them before long.

I later talked with the guard who shot Roger, and he told me he had no intentions of killing the boy and felt bad about its happening. He said that he was shooting in dim light and that the boy was zig-zagging and he could not be sure where his shots were going. This explanation, which he was not obliged to give, seemed plausible; and the fact that he visited Roger before he died and that the boy held no malice is further proof of his sincerity.

The story of Eddie Britt and Jerry Coburn is another example of friendship that burns out too quickly when "the blue chips are down."

These two friends had been in an isolation cell together for about six months. Both were considered dangerous, especially Britt. They had been planning a daring escape ever since they had first been locked up, and they were now ready to put it into operation. The bars had been sawed through for quite some time. They had been "soaped," and all that was needed for the job was a stormy night. It arrived.

The guard made his rounds and called in to the captain's office, and then he settled down for a few minutes rest. Snores and whines could be heard coming from the various cells, and occasionally a man who was having trouble living with a ghost would let out a short scream. However, in cell number three on the lower floor, Eddie Britt and Jerry Coburn had never been so wide awake—or so excited and determined.

Eddie lifted the bars out carefully and laid them beneath the slat bunk. He looked out to see if the keeper of the hothouse, which was just beneath the window, had removed the several panes of glass as he had been told to do. The opening was there, and Eddie, followed closely by Jerry, climbed out and dropped into the hothouse. Eddie went to a certain spot and came up with a long rope with a steel hook on one end. The two men then broke out of the little hothouse and, in the rain and darkness, made their way to the east wall, just halfway between the corner towers.

Eddie threw the hook over the wall, and miraculously it caught on the outside ledge. This was an omen of good luck to Eddie, and he began to scamper up the rope. Before he had reached the top, Jerry began the ascent. Just as Eddie rolled safely to the top of the wall, Jerry's hands slipped on the wet rope, and he plunged to the hard ground below, breaking a leg. The tower guards were alert now and began shooting down the wall. Eddie could have dropped to the outside and made good his escape, but he decided to take his pal with him or not go. He shouted for Jerry to hang on to the rope, and he began to pull him up. With bullets spraying all around him, Eddie managed to get the injured man to the top and then let him down outside. He then jumped and carried Jerry to a car that had been waiting at a certain spot every night for months.

Although a long and thorough search was made, no trace was found of the escapees. Law-enforcement officers were alerted all over the state, but it was several months before any line could be found giving a clue to the whereabouts of the two dangerous men. Then it was discovered that they were operating out of one of the larger cities and that most of the robberies and shootings in that area were the work of these two men. Finally, Eddie was positively identified as the man who shot a policeman, and the heat was really on. Several killings followed, and the law was able to tie Eddie to each one, but as yet could not pin a crime on Jerry.

Jerry was still with Eddie, however, and while he had not actually shot anyone, he was badly wanted. What the police did not know was that Jerry was becoming jittery and wanted out of the heat. Neither did Eddie suspect this. They planned a big job, and although Jerry had no heart for it, he agreed to go along. He thought he saw a chance to get out and help himself at the same time.

They kept their car in a garage near the uptown district, under assumed names, and it was the plan that Eddie would go and get the car during the evening hours, when there was less chance of being noticed. He was to return and pick up Jerry, and they would leave town and be at the scene of their job early the next morning.

As soon as Eddie left the apartment, Jerry packed his clothes, then went down to a corner drugstore and called a number. He talked briefly, left the store, and went back to the apartment, got his bags and called a taxi.

Eddie was just attempting to start the motor of his car when he noticed two officers coming in the front door. He hastily looked toward the back and saw that he was trapped. He did the only thing he could do—short of surrendering—he drew his gun and began shooting at the police. A short but bloody gun battle ensued, and when it was over, one policeman and Eddie were dead and several officers wounded. It was later reported that after Eddie was down and dying, one of the officers stood astraddle the outlaw's body and emptied his gun in the fallen man's face, saying, "You'll never kill another cop, you dirty rat." Eddie Britt had paid the terrible price of false friendship and trust. He had been sold out by a man whom he had once risked his own life to save.

What price friendship? It could be horrible, sudden death by a hostile law, or it could be worse—to have to live with the knowledge that you were a Judas.

One of the most ingenious and vicious plots ever conceived at this prison was known as "the Bomber's caper." It failed, but had it been carried out as planned, there would have been a holocaust fed by human bodies. One of the strange things about this caper was that most of the participants ordinarily were decent sorts of fellows who showed no signs of real viciousness.

The main hobby for convicts at one time was the making of rings and other items of celluloid. All combs and tooth-brushes were made of this material then, and it was permissible to work it into different souvenirs. It was even permissible to send out and buy sheets of the stuff, which was not recognized as dangerous. If the officials were aware that celluloid was very explosive, they ignored the fact, or didn't think of what might happen. But the cunning minds of the convicts conceived an idea that could possibly have been their key to freedom.

The first step was to accumulate a good supply of celluloid. This was no difficult chore. When they had what they thought was enough, they began shaving it all down into fine powder. They managed to get several steel pipes, about eight inches long and sealed at both ends. They then bored a hole in each tube and packed it with the fine powder. When it contained all that it would hold, a small bunch of sulphur match heads were packed in on top of the powder, just inside the hole. A fuse was inserted, and the opening packed tight. The result was a bomb of almost unbelievable power.

The bombs were kept in the mine, and one Tuesday, which was the usual day for shooting entries in the mine, they decided to try one out and see if it worked as the originator claimed it would. They discovered that these weapons were more potent than they had hoped for.

Things might have gone well for the ambitious men except for the fact that, as almost always, there was one who could not keep from letting others know how smart he was. The result? The vice squad swooped down and confiscated the bombs and the manufacturers. They later found out that the plan was to throw bombs in the towers and then to go over the wall. When the officials tried one of these bombs out on the frozen ground, they realized what a catastrophe had been averted.

All the participants in that project have left, and I have no idea whether or not more than one is still alive. However, I know that the main leader of the project is living. I met him some time back in another state. He was married, owned his own home, and was doing quite well. He said to me, "Boy, what a chump I was. I'm glad it came out as it did."

There have been many attempts to break out of the Lansing prison. Some were successful, but most were utter failures that resulted in death or additional time to serve. Most of those who did escape, however, have been accounted for, either by execution in other states or by violence while committing crime. I mention this now, because it is amazing how men will gamble away their freedom, then risk everything in an attempt to regain it.

I might point out that while such things could possibly happen today, it is less likely, due to the improvement in security methods. There is very little time when men are not under some sort of surveillance, but there always will be danger of such things happening as long as prisons exist. Anything that man can build, man can also destroy. Another reason why these things are not so apt to happen is because the convicts no longer have easy access to material and equipment with which to build deadly weapons. There are too many men serving time today who realize that any attempt to escape is detrimental to their chances of earning a legitimate release at the earliest possible moment. These men, while not necessarily finks, do let the troublemakers know that they will not react pleasantly to any outbreak that may hinder the chances of the general population. These attitudes help curb any ideas that might be stirred up in the warped and bitter minds of some narrow-minded prisoners. The attitude of most prisoners today has changed from one of "freedom at any cost."

The only way that men who have never known anything else but crime can be helped to change is by winning their confidence and convincing them that society not only wants them, but needs them. It is the job of the penologists to persuade men to want to change to a better way of life. If they cannot be made to want to become law-abiding citizens, no power, no punishment, no inducement, can bring it about. The old saying "You can lead a horse to water, but you can't make him drink" is certainly true in this case. It would be easier to make every human being go to church than it would to make a bad man be good.

There are very few of us who have served many years who haven't wondered at one time or another why we do the things we do. It is possible that we became too concerned with "why" and not concerned enough about how we are going to stop doing the things that get us into trouble. A doctor surely wouldn't allow a patient to die unattended while he looked for the cause of some unknown disease. It would do us little good to discover the why unless we had some idea of what to do about it. Of course, in medicine it is necessary to have some idea of what the trouble is before much can be done to cure the disease. However, the doctor usually does something to slow it down until the cause can be found. That is what must be done about the crime problem.

I believe the best bet, and the only hope of society in its struggle to make men want to understand and abide by the accepted customs and concepts of the society in which they must exist, is to help them to realize the folly of leaping headlong into the limelight instead of following an orderly and planned journey to success and happiness. This can be done only by helping them learn how to live, how to use the one feature that is conspicuous by its absence in almost all offenders—forethought. Unless men are taught about this important tool and inspired to make it a part of their every day life, about all that can be expected is recidivism—in big doses.

It does not take a brilliant person to mature mentally, but it does take a trained person to teach how it is accomplished. It is merely a changing of attitudes from negative to positive—a changing of our self-image from one of failure and inadequacy to one of being successful. We must learn to understand what the authorities mean when they tell us that we are "unique"—that we are different from every other person on earth. We are what we think we are, nothing more, nothing less. As a famous psychologist says, "You are not inferior, you are not superior—you are you."

We often hear men say, "I am too old to change now." When we hear that, we may be sure that we are hearing the voice of a very foolish and immature person. Mental and emotional maturity will enable us to control those urges that drive us to be destructive and will help us to have a sincere desire to be productive and successful. We will be better equipped to cope with the many problems which confront us in a world that is progressing more rapidly than we are learning how to live in it. We will be more apt to make the right decisions when we are faced with strife, prejudices, and hatreds. This is a frame of mind that can be reached by anyone with an ounce of moral strength and the ability to think honestly and to act accordingly. Age is not a factor in the appetency to be thoughtful and kind, or in the changing of the self-image. Age does not hinder us from seeing things from the viewpoint of others as well as ourselves, nor from admitting our faults when we find them—it does not take from us the courage to compromise with facts.

The most alarming phase of the crime problem today is juvenile delinquency. We should be very careful before condemning younger offenders. It is true that they are committing more and more vicious and senseless crimes—many without reason or real motive. We abhor this fact, and yet we must, in all fairness, ask ourselves this question—and answer it honestly. "Whose fault is it that these young people have thrown principle and caution to the wind and lost all regard for human life?"

We were all children at one time or another. That is one statement I can make without fear of contradiction. This being true, it might be well for us to spend a few moments in retrospection and to review, in all honesty, some of the things we did—or at least wanted to do—before judging the youngsters of today. How did we act? We acted like just what we were—juveniles. We all wanted a hero, someone we could emulate and look up to. Some of us found what we were looking for at home, but others had to find it elsewhere. It was the latter who usually wound up in trouble in later life.

If dad or mother were people that could give us pride and a feeling of trust and security, we stayed home and were contented to follow in their footsteps. If they were drunks and thieves, and if dad beat the family and starved them, we either went some other place or surrendered and accepted this sort of life until it eventually became a part of our existence. We became tolerant of it until we finally decided to "let the chips fall where they would." The constant association with good or bad will always result in some of it rubbing off.

Those of us who were forced to look outside the home for our idols did it with the best intentions. But where could we look in those days except in the "dime novels," the pool halls, and, at last, the saloons. We had little to choose from. We could pretend we were Jesse James or Wyatt Earp—or the more intellectual could pick a Horatio Alger character. Of course, no one from across the tracks ever dared do the latter. The choice a child makes is dependent to a large degree on which of the idols dad resembles the most.

There are a lot of questions parents should ask themselves before it is too late. "Have I ever invited my child to come to me with his problems? And if he has brought them to me, have I given him the attention I should have, or have I brushed him off, not realizing that even though his problem might seem trivial and unimportant to me, it was as big as a mountain to him? Have I ever made my boy or girl understand that when their problems got too heavy for them to carry, they could unload them on me?" Your honest answers to these questions may be the difference someday between your looking at your child through the bars of a jail or prison and looking on while he or she is acclaimed for some fine deed or accomplishment.

Not too long ago I had the opportunity—if it can be called that—of seeing a mother leave the prison after visiting her young son who had just killed another inmate. I wish every man and woman could have witnessed that scene. It was truly a "picture from life's other side." It was the side of sorrow, shame, heartbreak, utter despair. It was a real lesson in why every parent should take the lives of their children more seriously so that one day they will not have to ask, "Where did I fail?"

No matter what we do, not all youngsters will grow up to

be president, not even of the "rinky-dinks," but all can grow up to be respected, benevolent, and trustworthy human beings, credits to the community and joys to the ones who gave them life. However, they must be helped and guided over the rough, uncertain road and over the bumps they will encounter as they grow up. They must be made to believe that happiness is never found in a bottle, or in the leaves of a poisonous weed.

9

❖❖❖

What Leads Men
to Crime?

For in it things are done
That Son of God nor Son of Man
Ever should look upon!

DURING MY years of confinement I have met about every type
of criminal in existence. As I let my memory wander back, I
am a bit surprised to recall that in almost every case, the men
who committed the more important crimes were those who
were blessed with parents who were above reproach and were
among the ones most respected in the society of which they
were a part. I have wondered if this could be due to over-in-
dulgence? Did these parents try too hard to be kind and con-
siderate? Or did these parents allow themselves to be misled
into believing, as so many parents have, that their child just
could not be guilty of wrongdoing? Did they overlook the
little things, passing them off as insignificant and permitting
them to snowball into big crimes? Did they take with a grain
of salt the saying "Spare the rod and spoil the child"?

It is difficult to understand why many men, through lust
and greed, destine themselves to a life of bondage, to be hated
by the very scrapings from the same barrel they themselves
came from. Certainly it is not because they don't know better.
Any man who is able to live among people and function with

any degree of reason, who is able to do good work and to eat and sleep well, knows when he is doing wrong. It is either that he does not have a desire to live any better, or that he has never been shown how to grow up and think as adults should.

The Kansas "Million Dollar" bond scandal exemplifies that it is not always the kid from across the tracks that commits the biggest and most harmful crime. With two possible exceptions, the men involved in this crime were of prominent families, and one of these two men was an elected, trusted official of the state.

Several bankers were involved in this steal, one of whom committed suicide when he saw that the jig was up. His son received a long sentence, and so did several of the errand boys, but all of them combined did not serve as much time as the average man serves for a common robbery.

The banker's son worked in the mine at his own request. He knew he could buy "good time" from the miners, who received two days and fifty cents for all coal over their task. He had a job tending a switch. This consisted of sleeping all day on a straw pallet and having his meals carried to him. When this job fell through, he was assigned one where he slept out and had his own house. He went to the kitchen each day and picked up the best steaks and whatever he needed to go with it. He lived like a king.

These men lived on what was called "banker's row" and dined at the "banker's table" in the kitchen. No one was eligible for this treatment unless he had stolen thousands of dollars from poor people who trusted him with their life's savings. These bankers, and we had a lot of them at that time, usually received a three-year sentence, regardless of how much money they had stolen. These special guests had men to make their bunks and sweep their cells, and they ate the very best of food. Their daily menu was usually something like ham and eggs, fruit juice, toast, cereal, and coffee for breakfast; short orders for lunch; and fine steaks for dinner. The waiters were paid by these privileged characters, and paid well.

Not being a member of the inner sanctum, I do not know all the details concerning this "super highway robbery," but I do know what happened to the men who pulled the job after they came here. They had what I like to call a bird's nest on the ground. I know that on at least one occasion, one of these men was permitted to dress up and go out on the town in Kansas City.

The banker's son was soon a free man, and according to reports, lived in luxury until his death a short time ago. He even bought a herd of elephants. I don't know what for, unless he needed them to carry around the loot he stole from the taxpayers of Kansas.

Many strange things have happened behind these walls, and one of the strangest was the murder of Jim Crow. Jim was a likable character, but he was also unpredictable. He was a known thief, a loudmouth, and an all-around pest; and yet he had something about him that demanded affection and fellowship. He was harmless, also useless, and if his killers had ever been found, it is hard to tell what terrible things might have happened to them. It was not altogether the killing that rankled everyone, it was the gruesome way in which it was done. The general opinion was that Jim probably needed what he got, but he deserved a more dignified death than he received.

At the baseball games, which we were permitted to attend then, due to the efforts of the ladies of Kansas (Bless 'em), Jim was one of the home team's most ardent fans. He was the only one who had a reserved seat, and he yelled and raised as much disturbance as anyone. But even there, Jim's kleptomania sometimes took over. If a player happened to lose his cap while running and was a bit slow picking it up, Jim had it, and that was the last anyone would ever see of that piece of apparel. He also pilfered from the cells, and

would leave his "calling card" occasionally, in the form of—
well, he left it on the blanket. He was always the first awake
in the morning, and he made sure everyone else was awake by
clamoring outside a window. He yacked and shouted a lot,
but never said anything. Of course, you have already guessed
—Jim was a crow.

I said that Jim was well liked. Well, he was by most men.
However, it is obvious that he had at least one enemy. Whoever the culprit was, he must have really hated Jim, judging
from the method he used to get rid of him. He figured out
some way to get Jim to eat a mixture that was saturated with
cathartic pills. Whatever this concoction was, it was powerful. When we found Jim after a three day search, he was in an
old sewer pipe down beind the twine plant. He was in terrible condition and suffering intense pain. We did what we
could, but it was no use. Jim died not only a painful death
but also a busy one right up to the bitter end.

It is interesting to note the many pets adopted by men in
prison. There have been birds of all kinds, skunks, cats, rabbits, rats, pigeons, mules, dogs—even cockroaches. And one of
the easiest ways to get hurt was to mistreat one of the pets. It
is rather strange that convicts are the tenderest men on earth
when it comes to an animal or bird and some insects. I have
often wondered if it isn't sort of refreshing to most of these
men to know that there is one living thing they can truly call
friend and can trust.

A cat called Tom the Fink was one of the pets content to
spend his life in prison with men who went out of their way
to treat him as another prisoner and protect him with their
lives. It was considered almost high treason in those days to
be caught with any food or equipment for cooking it. But
most of the fellows had a hot plate and a stinger.* They

* An electrical device that can be put in a cup or pan of liquid to heat the
contents.

would connive to get groceries from the kitchen, and it was a certainty that every evening, at a given time, the odor of frying potatoes and bacon and the strong, satisfying aroma of coffee could be noticed. The guard seldom made any real effort to catch these gourmets, but if he happened along and caught a man in the act, it was "shame on him."

Almost invariably, about the time the food was ready, the Fink would show up. He would sit outside the "hot" cell and lick his chops. If the occupants fed him, he would go about his business and look for another sucker. But woe be unto the ones who ignored him or tried to drive him away. He would get away out on the edge of the run and start howling like a banshee until the guard came running. But in spite of the fact that he was a fink, he was thought a lot of and in fact was the only one of the finger men who was safe in stir.

Although education was not considered important by most men in those days, there were a few who realized that perhaps their only hopes lay in this direction. I happened to be one of those, and I began a long struggle that is still going on. I have never faltered or slowed down in my determination to do something about the fifth-grade education I had when I first went to prison.

We did have a little spare time when things began to improve. The only problem was how to get permission to pursue the project. The only literature available was the Bible and other religious material. Several of us decided to do the best we could with this type of matter, some of us feeling that it might help us in more ways than one. The policy was to keep the ignorant, ignorant and to destroy the educated man's will and desire. It was pointed out that we were sent here to do a sentence at hard labor, not to get a college education. For these reasons, any kind of studying was frowned upon.

In spite of the fact that it was a beef to get caught, we would get down on the floor at night after the lights were out, with a piece of wrapping paper, or whatever kind we could pick up during the day, and a stub of pencil and study reading and spelling. We felt that we were capable of having more knowledge, although we were not sure what we wanted it for. It was very difficult to understand the writing in the Bible, but since it had to be concentrated on to make any sense, it is likely it did good in more ways than one. I did gain a better understanding of religion than I would have had otherwise. Finally I decided to see if I could buy a textbook of some kind. I inquired and found out what book would be the best, then went to see the deputy warden. I explained my mission and told the deputy that I felt I could better myself a little while serving time. He looked at me as if I was asking for a reprieve from the death sentence, leaned back in his chair, and roared, "Buy a book? Hell no, you can't buy a book. You're too damn smart now—and if you ain't smart, you ain't gonna be." That ended that idea for the time being.

A few months later, we heard of an old guard here who, believe it or not, had a college degree of some kind—in agriculture, I think. But that was more education than anyone else that we knew possessed. We approached the old man and put our proposition to him. He was interested and said he would see what he could do. He did take the matter up, and to our surprise, refused to take no for an answer. He stayed on the ball and finally began to get it rolling. He was turned down at the prison, but he had some friends that were influential in the powerful political circles that existed in Kansas at that time, and the matter was referred to the governor, who, like most governors of the times, realized the futility of resisting pressure and issued a directive that such classes be permitted so far as was consistent with security and production.

The arrangements were made. It was proclaimed that classes would be held two days a week in the old hospital wards. These classes would teach the fundamentals of the basic subjects, and it would be possible for a person to attain an eighth-grade education, or a reasonable facsimile thereof. One convict was good at shorthand and was willing to teach it. However, very few of us knew longhand too well, so he didn't get any students for a long time. A younger guard volunteered his spare time to help with the classes, and for a time it looked as if everything was going to work out all right. There was a run on the deputy warden's office by men seeking night jobs so that they could enroll in school. I was one of the lucky ones.

It wasn't long before the program began to hit snags, as is usual in the penitentiary. The opponents of the project, who composed the higher echelon, began to have urgent need for the teachers in other places and managed to find excuses to keep the pupils working overtime on their jobs. Soon the class fell apart entirely. We had classes only occasionally. This was better than no class at all, so we did the best we could.

The men who did desire a better education were not treated as close relatives by any means. They were arrested for anything—sometimes nothing—and put out of circulation. In a way this was good. It taught the men who were sincere in their desires, to be alert, use good judgment, and be patient. Finally the expected happened. The school was discontinued on the pretext that there was not enough help available to carry on the classes and to maintain security.

For the next few years we did the best we could with what we had, and we were surprised to notice that although the progress was slow, we had learned quite a bit. I have often wondered what might have happened to these eager men of yesteryear if they had been fortunate enough to have had the marvelous educational facilities in the prison today. Who knows? Some of us might have become teachers, lawyers, or even doctors, instead of what we are. At least I like to think of the possibilities.

The officials had the same negative attitude toward religion. It was tolerated but not embraced. However, it was the few sincere and compassionate people whom the chaplain managed to bring in here that led to many of the wonderful privileges existent today. In spite of the jeers and opposition from the officials, these sincere and faithful people came Sunday after Sunday and did their best to inspire the pitifully small group who dared attend services and risk ridicule from both the guards and the convicts who lacked the intestinal fortitude to seek what they needed, and in most cases really wanted. The feeling was that anyone who attended church services was either a "rapo" or some kind of nut. The basis of the opposition was "Why did you wait until you got in prison to become a churchgoer?" Apparently it did not strike these critics that many of the churchgoers were sincere and wanted to seek strength with which to effect a change in their attitudes and to learn how to live a better life. It is true beyond doubt that some of those who attended church had only one thought in mind—to get a good reputation for the benefit of the parole board. In those days very few paroles were granted. So few, in fact, that unless a man was serving a long sentence, he didn't even bother to go to the board. The applicant had to pay to see the board, and it didn't seem worthwhile.

It did seem that most of the men who carried around Bibles and preached religion were men convicted of rape or incest. However, I always felt that if anyone on this earth needed God, it was these men. Whether or not it helped many of them, I cannot truthfully say, but I do know of several that it certainly did not help. One of these was "Preacher" Jones.

Preacher was serving sentences for sodomy and other related crimes, and was also one of the most energetic members of the religious movement in the prison. He was also a firm believer in "not letting the right hand know what the left hand was doing." He carried his Bible in one hand and allowed the other to roam over the anatomy of every young boy he could get close to. But he did know the Bible. In fact, he came closer to converting me than any bona-fide preacher ever did, before I discovered—just in time—what a character he was. Old Preacher had a lot of faith—such as it was. It was permissible then to grow a beard, and he let his whiskers grow for several months, saying, "I know St. Peter will open the gates, and I am going to let my whiskers grow until he does." His whiskers were getting rather thick when something happened—I suppose he and St. Peter had a misunderstanding of some sort. He came out one morning with his face shaved clean. I asked him what happened, and he replied, "Oh, the hell with St. Peter! He ain't gonna open them gates."

A new man, perhaps as old as Preacher, was moved into his cell one time. He knew nothing of the nefarious doings of Preacher, and all went well until late in the night. Then the cellhouse guard heard the man shouting for help. "Come and get this guy," he was yelling. "He is trying to get in bed with me. Man, get away from me! I'm a man—not a woman."

The guard arrived in time, and he unlocked the door and made the offender come out on the tier. Preacher was in his underwear, but had his Bible under his arm. The guard asked him what he meant, trying a thing like that, and Preacher replied, "So help me, boss, the Lawd done tole me to do it. I just had to do what he tole me."

"Yeah?" the guard said. "Well, what do you think the Lord is telling me to do with you?"

"I don't know," Preacher replied, "but I know the Lawd don't hold with no whuppin'."

I must explain that all the men who professed their Christian beliefs while here were not of this stripe. Many were sincere, realized their real need for spiritual guidance, and never deviated from this belief as long as they were here. I don't know what happend to all of them after they left, but I met one that I knew, in another part of the country, many years later. What I discovered about this man made me feel proud that I had been one of his supporters back in the days of "tribulations." I found that although he had received practically no publicity, he had been responsible for leading more men to the "mourner's bench" than most men who had spent a lifetime in the ministry. He was happy and told me that he wanted no publicity—no eulogy. He felt that this might be detrimental to his ministry. He was content to do his job and get his reward from the One Whom he was happy to serve. I was especially happy for this man, because I felt that he had done a lot for me. It was gratifying to see him doing the thing he wanted to do—preaching the gospel.

So I say again that those brave people who came here, and fought for the right to do so, in order to offer men religion are to be commended. It was not any easy task, nor was it without its disappointments and heartbreaks. They had not only the skeptical convicts to contend with, but also the belligerent officials who believed it was a waste of time to try and teach convicts anything good. These people faced these problems with fortitude and faith and patience, the characteristics of true Christians. I say that wherever these good people may be now, they can somehow know that the wonderful work they did here has not been forgotten, nor will it ever be. They brought peace of mind to many men who otherwise might have died in torment and in agony.

If the appearance of the religious pioneers had no other effect, it was beneficial psychologically. It has seemed to me as I have kept a pretty close watch on the men with whom I have been associated over the years that when a man finds himself at a dead end, he is more receptive to applied psychology than is the man who enjoys smooth sailing. Perhaps this is because the man who is at his wits' end realizes that he must begin to have faith in something he can't see, rather than to go on demanding proof for everything before accepting it. Maybe he is of the opinion that he must try everything that promises release or escape from the precarious position he has allowed his mind to fall into.

I had a good friend here who became obsessed with the idea that he was dangerously ill. Every morning he would come to me, stick his tongue out, and say, "Look at my tongue. I'm really in bad shape. If I don't get something done, I won't live another year." He even began to look peaked and pale, but somehow I just couldn't believe that he had anything organically wrong with him. He did not have that appearance. I had read a good deal about disease and also about psychology, and while I knew I was not an authority on either, I came to the conclusion that my friend was actually "dying of good health." I decided to try my hand at psychology and "bogus" medicine.

It took me some time to figure out just what I was going to do. I knew that this fellow had absolute faith in anything I said, and this made the job easier. In fact, he thought I was about the smartest man on earth (and who was I to challenge his opinion?). The deputy had once told me the same thing—in different words.

As soon as I knew the direction I wanted to go, I looked Frank up on the yard. I said, "Frank, I didn't tell you before because I didn't want to worry you, but I think I should tell you my opinion. I have been pretty sure all along that you are a very sick man. I saw a man one time with the same looks and symptoms you have, and he was suffering from a rare disease that is almost always fatal unless you get the proper treatment. Doctors know little about this ailment, because it has appeared so seldom and then only in isolated areas— among the Indians and other small groups. However, don't let it worry you too much, because it happens that I knew an old Indian who gave me the recipe for an absolutely positive cure for this particular disease. But I must ask you not to breathe a word of this to anyone. It is very secret, and besides it's against the rules."

Frank eagerly agreed and was very anxious for me to give him the medicine. I told him, "Now, it will take me several days to get the ingredients I need and put them together, so I want you to be patient, and when I do give you the medicine,

I want you to follow the directions I give you. If you don't do this, then the cure will not be certain." Frank swore he would do just as I wanted him to do.

I waited a few days, then made up my concoction. I shaped five pills, took them to Frank, and said, "I want you to take one of these at bedtime and one before each meal. Keep these hidden, and when they are gone, come back and I will give you five more—that will be all you will have to take. You'll feel like a new man."

It was several days before I saw Frank again. When I did, I almost passed out. He was out on the baseball diamond, playing just as energetically as anyone else, and he was apparently having a big time. This was something that no one had ever seen before. Frank had always dragged around and seemed all in. When he saw me standing by the fence, he came over —all smiles—and said, "Boy, you sure know what you are doing. That is the best medicine I ever took, and it really went to work fast. I noticed a difference the very first night. You ought to get a patent on that stuff—it really works!" I decided he didn't need the other five pills I had made, so I fed them to the pigeons—they were made of bran flakes and syrup. Frank kept after me to patent them, and I told him I was sure that this medicine had already helped many people and would probably keep on doing so.

Frank never had a relapse and became one of the most active men in the prison. This encouraged me, and it was not long before I had a chance to try my psychological talents in another way. This was also the case of a good friend, a young fellow who worked with me in the kitchen. He was almost obsessed with the desire to someday become a great chef. He had talent, and it seemed to me that he had almost everything he needed to make his dreams come true. But he had a tendency to be ambitious and elated at one moment, and in a blue funk the next. This, I felt, was not the symptom of a serious mental disorder, but simply a case of no self-confidence. I wondered what he would do with a direct challenge, and the more I toyed with the idea, the more I became convinced that if I acted just right, I might be able to help him find whatever it was that he lacked. As I pondered how to approach the problem, I thought "What could be a better challenge than to go on and become what you want to become?" It had never become a challenge to this boy—only a desire and a hope. I reasoned that unless he was helped to find himself now, he might go through life as so many other men have done—just a step away from success and unable to take that step. Maybe I could make him take that step and give him the momentum he needed. I knew I was going to try, and I also knew that this would be different and perhaps more dangerous than anything I had yet attempted. I knew I would be risking our friendship. He might even come to hate me. However, if it served the purpose, I could endure even that.

It was, and is, my opinion that all men have a flame going at some time in their lives, but some allow it to burn out and never bother to relight it. If this was the trouble with my friend, I had hopes that maybe I could furnish the spark needed to make the flame rise again. If I could not do this, there seemed to be a good chance that a great talent would be wasted and another life would prove unproductive.

I began slowly, by daring him to accomplish what he wanted to accomplish and by dropping hints that I knew he could never do it. These hints were what did the job. Then I said, "Maybe you just might as well forget it. You could never be a chef; you just haven't got what it takes. It takes guts to face those kind of odds, and I don't think you've got them. You couldn't stand the gaff. So why don't you try something you can handle. I don't know what that would be, except perhaps stealing, and I don't think you would be too good at that."

I will never forget how he glared at me. I thought for a moment that he might try my air,* but he turned and walked

* Fight me.

away. He never came around me much after that, but I noticed that he was working harder, studying every book he could find on the subject of cooking. His boss told me that he had suddenly become a different boy. He was seldom seen on the yard, and he worked every chance he got. He liked to experiment, and his boss said that he come up with some fine dishes.

At last it came time for him to be released. He had become a fine cook, and I was proud of him, although I didn't tell him so. He came to me on that last morning and said, "Thanks, pal, you'll never know what you did for me." But he was wrong. I did know that I had been permitted to be a little help in giving a boy a push in the right direction. I felt sure that no prison would ever hold him again.

Many years later, I was out in the Pacific Northwest and was on the pork.* I needed a job badly. I heard that a railroad wanted men in the culinary department. I went to apply for a job.

The clerk told me that the superintendent would see me presently, but he looked at my none-too-natty appearance as if to say, "But I don't think he needs any scavenger men." In a few minutes he motioned me to go in, and as I walked into the plush office, I remember I had a peculiar, unexplainable feeling—as if something out of the ordinary was about to happen. It couldn't have been that I expected to be thrown out. That would not have been out of the ordinary.

The well-dressed man behind the big desk was busy with some paper work and didn't look up for a moment, and when he did, I almost fell flat on my face. It was my friend of long ago, and he was just as astounded as I was. We both just stared. When he recovered, he arose quickly and walked around the desk and grabbed me by the hand. I was still in a stupor. I couldn't believe what I was seeing.

* On the bum.

"Where in the world did you come from?" he asked. "You are the last person I expected to see out here, but believe me, I'm glad you are here."

I slowly drifted back to earth and discovered that I still had a voice. I said, "Well, if you are surprised, what do you think I am? I would not have been nearly so unnerved if I had found Adolf Hitler sitting behind that desk."

He called his clerk and said, "I will be busy the rest of the day, Melvin, I just found an old friend." The clerk sniffed at me, turned his big nose up, and walked out with an air that somehow told me that he thought his boss must have taken up the study of old relics and fossils.

We talked for a while, and then he took me to his fine home, where I met his beautiful wife and two lovely children. I thought I must be living a scene from one of Horatio Alger's books. This just did not make sense, and yet it was true. And as the evening wore on, I discovered that I was just a little proud that I had had a small part in this drama—this wonderful turnaround of a man who accepted a challenge which proved to be the incentive he needed. Here was absolute proof that a man can achieve his heart's desire if he learns to change his self-image from one of failure to one of success, to set a definite goal, and to believe in it with all his heart. He can do almost anything if he realizes the terrific power that is inside him and learns that every human being has access to that power.

As we sat in his home that evening and sipped our soft drinks, he recalled the time that I had so deliberately insulted him and thereby caused him to vow that he would do what I told him he could never do. He told me that inwardly he had a hunch that I was purposely trying to antagonize him, but that it was some time before he figured out why. By the time he did figure it out, he was inspired to the point that his study and work became a habit. He admitted that he had contemplated giving me a bust in the nose, but something told him that the "Wise Old Owl" had some reason for doing what he did. I thanked him for the new monicker—and incidentally, I have been called that in many quarters since that time. When he thanked me, I told him that he should remember that his help came from One far greater than me, or any mortal man, and that he should give his thanks to Him.

On these two occasions my psychological efforts seemed to be a big success. However, my batting average went down a long way the next time I went to bat. This shows that what will work for good in some cases can backfire and do harm in others, especially when experimenting with things as complex as psychology.

I once knew a young fellow who at the age of twenty-three had been convicted of highway robbery, paroled, and then arrested again for the same thing. He didn't seem to be a vicious boy. He had a good education and was well liked in the prison, and as far as I know, outside. One day after he had been told that he had made another parole, he said that he was going to make good this time, no more horsing around, as he called it. He swore that he was all through with stealing and all related occupations. As I look back now, I can't help but believe he really meant it. However, at the time I had many doubts. When I think now what happened, I wish I had kept my big mouth shut. But I thought maybe he needed a challenge. At that time I didn't know how well my other challenge had worked, but I decided to present this boy with one. I said, "No, you won't make it—you won't behave yourself. You can't. You don't know how, and you don't want to very badly. You'll do just like you've always done. You think you're Jesse James, and anyhow you don't have the nerve to go out and make good. It can be done, but not by you."

He stayed out about three months and was returned for the same crime—robbery. He said, "So what? No one believed in me. Even you didn't think I could go straight." This has always bothered me. I cannot help but feel that I contributed to this boy's downfall, when my desire was to help him. This, however, is an example of what can happen when a man lets the beliefs of others overshadow his own self-confidence and cause him to lower the true estimate of his self-image. It is also proof of the known, but little heeded, fact that there is no rule that will apply to all human beings. What will work with one will not necessarily work with another.

There is one thing about the average criminal that should be remembered. He is unstable and usually very sensitive. He realizes his shortcomings and his low stature in society, and he tries to present at all times an attitude of being content to remain just what he is, a round peg trying to fit into a square hole. In reality, he would give most anything to learn how to be a respected and trusted member of his society. This may be called an inferiority complex, but to me it is the inability to cope with a puzzling situation.

I doubt very much if there are very many men who are criminals because they want to be. They have either permitted themselves to become involved without realizing their mistake before it was too late, or they have been unable to reason themselves out of what they thought was a serious situation.

There is another type of criminal that has become so exposed to crime that it seems to him there is no other way to live. He never has learned how respectable people live. The only existence he has known is one that is the result of a belligerent world, full of rules and regulations made just for him. He has never learned that there is a proper and orderly way to gain recognition. It would be impossible, so long as he has such an attitude and wallows in such ignorance, to get him to anticipate the thrill of fishing, golf, baseball, and other sports, or to understand that by participating in such sports, he could enjoy an even greater challenge than he could ever get from a heist or a prowl.

The most misled of all are those who think there is something glamorous about being called a hood. They cannot understand that when respectable people look at a criminal with staring eyes, it is not with admiration, but with pity or utter contempt.

It is just as necessary to teach the criminal how to live right as it is to teach a baby how to walk and talk. Actually, the average so-called criminal is nothing more than a child who either has never learned to live properly or has neglected to practice it over the years. These men can be put back on the right track if properly and sincerely guided and taught. If it is not worth the effort to teach and counsel those wayward men, then society will just have to go on paying the terrific price it has been paying for so many years, with no promise of dividends. It is sheer folly for society to say, "We can't afford to spend time and money on these misfits. Let them pay for their crimes." What do they mean, "Let the criminal pay"? It is society who must pay—through the nose—as the crowds did who came to see the hanging of the man Dickson, mentioned earlier. If it is worth the millions the taxpayers lose every year to see men deprived of their freedom—or life—without doing anything to try and change the situation, then about all society can look forward to is a larger bill every year; and eventually it will see the situation get so far out of hand that remedy will be out of the question. Punishment alone has never been effective in slowing down crime, and it never will be. It must be accompanied by teaching and inspiring men to do better.

10

The Day All Hell
Broke Loose

Like two doomed ships that pass in storm
We had crossed each other's way: ...

YOU HAVE read of many strange personalities in this book. In prison the strange happenings never cease to exist and the strange characters never fail to perform. The following is one of the most colorful and exciting of them all. It concerns the lives of two men who, after experiencing the intrigues, heartbreaks, and shames of crime, were later drawn together to end their careers in prison and in death. It was the beginning of the end for Bill LaTrasse, whom we mentioned earlier, and Harry "Red" Downs, his accomplice in a caper which I refer to as "The Day All Hell Broke Loose." I will relate the story just as Red and Bill told it to me on separate occasions. I must accept it as being basically true, because of the similarity of the happenings as given by each man and by the reports I read at the time. I also was well acquainted with both men and knew much about them that very few other people know.

The tragedy of one's life may appear in many guises. Perhaps an unrequited love, or a severe handicap, such as being born blind, deaf, or deformed. It may come in the form of a subconscious feeling of guilt, a negative picture of one's inner self, or frustration at not being able to relieve the intense suf-

179

fering of a loved one. The last of these was no doubt an important factor in the checkered life of Red Downs. But regardless of the cause, it took its inevitable toll of human life, suffering, and heartache.

Harry's father was a Spanish-American War veteran and as this story begins, was a saloon keeper in St. Joseph, Missouri. His mother, a very religious lady, was Alma Gertrude Colemen before her marriage. On May 9, 1901, Mrs. Downs gave birth to a girl. As a result of this birth, and that of Red seventeen months later, the mother became ill and grew steadily worse.

In spite of this stroke of bad luck, the family led a fairly happy life until the medical expenses became almost too heavy to bear. At this time, Mr. Downs, as so many men before him had done, made the mistake of becoming his own best customer at the saloon. He, like others, was misled into believing that the solution to all problems comes in a bottle. He discovered how wrong this thinking was, however, when the saloon was gone, along with Mrs. Downs's ability to use her limbs at all.

Suddenly and unexpectedly, Mr. Downs sobered up and took a job as a stock clerk for the Jones Store Company in Kansas City, Missouri. The family, which had been separated for some time, now came back together and lived at 3714 Euclid Avenue. The children went to Horace Mann School and attended Sunday School at the Christian Science Church at Thirty-First and Troost Avenue. At this time Red was already a member of the kid gangs which frequented the park at Thirteenth and Summit streets. Mr. Downs entered politics about this time and became a precinct man in the First Ward, a democratic stronghold of Tom Pendergast on the old west side, in the vicinity of Sixteenth and Jefferson streets.

Red's crime career began with the robbery of a sporting-goods warehouse at Sixth and Washington streets. The boys were caught, and six of them received two- and four-year sentences at Booneville, Missouri. Red and several of his companions were given bench paroles. This did not dampen the spirit of the young hoodlum, and he was soon again in custody for the robbery of a bawdy house at 1219 Wyandotte Street. This, according to Red, was an "on-the-spur-of-the-moment job." These young prowlers were on the alert. They happened to be near when the police raided the house of ill repute, and as the law went out the front door with the prisoners, the boys went in the back door, intent on robbery. They carried off clothing, jewelry and other valuables, as well as the coins from two player pianos. They were arrested, and because of the political affiliations of Harry's father and the fact that the case was a bit shaky for lack of concrete evidence, the case was quashed when the boys kept tight lips. "This," said Red, "taught me the value of keeping my mouth shut."

His next big mistake was to quit school and lie about his age in obtaining a permit to work. He began working for the various messenger services, which, I know from experience, contributed to his eventual downfall. These dens were hotbeds of crime and perversion, where young boys came into daily contact with the underworld and its inhabitants. No day passed that a messenger of those days didn't see the inside of the many sporting houses and receive propositions from every type of sexual pervert. He carried narcotics to the users (they could be bought in any drugstore by anyone), and in this way many innocent and hard-working lads experienced their first "kiss of the poppy."

For the next few years Red divided his time as a candy butcher at the old Gaiety Theatre, a taxi-driver, teamster, soda-dispenser, and in learning how to become a first-class hood. Red helped to install the first automatic telephone in Kansas City, while working for the Home Telephone Company. He also drove the first taxicab to sit on the corner of Twelfth and Wyandotte. The cab was owned by Carl Carmelle, and it was this taxicab that finally put the messenger services out of business.

When prohibition came into effect, whiskey prices were hiked to $100 a case, and almost every home in Kansas City had a cache of the stuff in the basement. This made for a good prowl, with ready money available at all times. Red became a partner in crime with Kansas City and half its citizens in taking over the liquor interests and moving them into the underworld of politics, graft, and crime.

Until the age of eighteen, Harry was nothing more than an understudy to the big wheels, but from then on he blossomed out into a full-fledged mobster on his own. He got his first big bust in 1922, when he was charged with first-degree robbery. He and an accomplice were positively identified as the men who robbed Robert Esties of 8,000 dollars at his cigar store at Twelfth and Genesee. John De Salvo, sometimes known as "King of little Italy," signed a twenty-thousand-dollar bond for the men. Joe Glyward was their lawyer. They spent six days in jail and never did go to trial. Again politics played its role in the game of crime.

The word that was out on Twelfth Street was, "Don't get caught in Kansas." To get arrested in Kansas City, Missouri, for any crime was hardly more than a routine matter—arrest, bail, and release—if you knew the right people. Bold daylight robberies were not uncommon, and murders went unsolved. For instance, the Denny Chester murder trial, one of the largest ever held in Kansas City, Missouri, produced a parade of alibi witnesses that swamped—literally overpowered—the prosecution's attempt to bring justice to bear. Chester was speedily acquitted. Joe Glyward was the defense lawyer. He carried the keys to the city, and fix was the master key.

Two men, both underworld characters, were the cause of Red's first fall in prison. Floyd Dudley and George Willis, according to Red, were his downfall. He was arrested for the daylight holdup of a payroll at Joe Howard's cigar store at 6

Kansas Avenue in Kansas City, Kansas. In spite of the fact that this happened in Kansas, where convictions were not hard to come by, the prosecution, according to Red's own statement, had to frame the evidence in order to convict him.

Willis and Dudley, who turned state's evidence, testified that the tip-off man for the job was John Hagen, former head of the Midwest Detective Agency. He was alledged to have received the usual ten percent for the inside information which made the job possible. Hagen, after Willis and Dudley confessed the full details of the robbery, fled to Mexico till the heat was off. He did not return to Kansas City until the fix was in. His lawyer was Jesse James, Jr., son of the infamous outlaw. Hagen never came to trial on the charge.

In the allegedly true confession made to the Kansas City, Kansas, police, Dudley and Willis gave a list of at least fifty names of gunmen, thieves, and prominent businessmen, including many policemen and officials, who they claimed were directly involved in, and named to be a part of, a crime ring with vast connections operating in Kansas City, Missouri—and throughout the midwest. This was before the installation of state police in either Kansas or Missouri, and before the government had made it unlawful to cross state lines in the commission of a crime.

Harry and a former U.S. postal clerk, Earl Welch, received ten to twenty-one years, while Dudley and Willis received one to five years for the Howard robery. The holdup had netted the daylight bandits 2,072 dollars. Dudley admitted that his part in the job was to sack up the money and that in his haste he had overlooked ten thousand dollars that had just been brought from the bank and hidden under some newspapers.

Red spent ten months in the Wyandotte County Jail, two thousand dollars, and three taxicabs, trying to beat the rap. Welch did about three years in the Kansas State Penitentiary. Willis was later tried for bank robbery and given ten to fifty years, and Dudley served about seventeen months and was paroled. Red was the youngest of the gang at twenty-one, and he served five years before receiving a time cut and eventual parole. Red Downs always claimed that he was innocent of this crime—he still does—and although he was a model prisoner, he came out a very bitter young man. When the opportunity presented itself—or when he sought it— he entered the field of crime, according to his own admission, with a vengeance.

When he was released from Lansing, Red went back to Kansas City to live with his father. This didn't work out. They could not get along, and Red drifted back into the rackets with a former inmate of the Kansas State Penitentiary, "Boot Nose" Miller. These two, occasionally assisted by other thugs, pulled robberies in and around Kansas City, until apprehended and sentenced to 450 years on nine counts of first-degree robbery—fifty years on each count to run concurrently, or as some prisoners put it, aggravatingly. These sentences were the most severe ever meted out in Jackson County, Missouri.

In 1929 the Missouri State Penitentiary at Jefferson City was loaded with three or four thousand convicts. "Jeff City," as it is commonly called, was also known as one of the "Twin Hells"; the Kansas State Penitentiary being the other. Jeff, like Lansing, was undoubtedly one of the most brutal, backward, and shameful prisons in the United States. For sheer brutality, practiced by more or less ignorant and sadistic guards, these two prisons had no equal.

According to Red, he was paroled to Kansas City in 1942, but there appears to be some mistake here. In view of the report that follows, I must assume that the year of parole was 1941 instead of 1942 as Red claims. I do know that the date given for the following incident is accurate.

After Red had been out about a year on parole and had kept a good record, he met Bill LaTrasse, whom he had known in the Kansas prison and also at Jefferson City. Bill had fallen from his high position among the nation's top criminals of the day. He was a skid-row bum. He had received his sentence at Jefferson City for the holdup of a small hamburger stand, which netted him a few dollars. When Red met him, he was about to fall into the same rut. He was drinking whatever he could mooch or steal.

It is interesting to note that both these men came from homes where religion played a big part. Both Bill's and Red's mothers were God-fearing women and did their very best to bring their boys up right. After Bill's first real crime, it is reported that his mother kept a light burning in the window every night of her life in the hopes that Bill would come home and behave himself.

According to all reports available, neither of these men was mentally disturbed. They had no homosexual tendencies, and they were well liked by almost everyone who knew them. They were trustworthy as far as their dealings with fellow criminals, but both had a strong love for easy money—they could not resist the urge to make a fast buck on a heist or by any other nefarious method. Bill was an excellent leatherworker and shoemaker, and Red was an electrician who enjoyed the arts. In prison he spent nearly all his spare time reading and studying.

Being alike in so many ways, it may have been inevitable that Bill and Red become a team. In any case, they worked out a scheme for their operation, and as Red later told me, "It was Bill's idea of perfect crime—a way to commit robbery without breaking the law. We thought out the details and then went to work." (Apparently Red and Bill were laboring under the gross misapprehension that it was legal to rob an illegal operation of any kind—especially gambling. It is just as much robbery to hold up an illegal dice game as it is to heist a bank. The law does not protect any type of robbery.)

Topeka was the first town to experience the work of these

self-styled legal robbers. The boys robbed a dice game and netted about three thousand dollars, which in those days wasn't hay. A second game of this kind brought eighteen hundred dollars, and the third, Frank Magner's dice game in a back room of the Plaza Bar in Parsons, Kansas, brought death to two men and doom to two others.

When the robbery was planned, it was decided to enlist the aid of John Bachman, twenty-two-year-old nephew of Bill's, to drive the getaway car. The job was cased for several weeks to make sure that there would be no slip-ups, and the getaway route was laid out. When all seemed to be foolproof, the date was set, and the men prepared their weapons and ran over the plans, much as football players plan a game.

On the appointed night, business was even better than usual. This assured the bandits of a good haul. This job was really going to pay off—and how. Bill lead the way into the back room where the game was in progress, followed closely by Red. Bachman, who was the driver and lookout man, stepped into the hallway outside, where he could see and hear all that took place. When they were in their prearranged places, they shouted, in unison, "This is a stickup. Don't try to be heroes, and no one will get hurt." The players obeyed and were promptly lined up against a wall. Bill went for the banker's money, stuffing bundles of money into the front of his shirt. Harry shook the individual players down and relieved them of their valuables. After the money had been collected—to the last dollar—and they started to go, all hell broke loose in the form of two foolish men who apparently were more concerned with their money than with their lives.

A barber by the name of Tom Miller and his son, Clint Miller, attacked Bill and Harry as they backed toward the door. Clint Miller, a former football player and well-known barroom brawler of one-punch fame, threw a punch at Red, which he ducked. As Red shuffled aside, Clint's momentum carried him toward Bill, thus placing him between two deadly fires. Just as Clint threw a punch at Bill, both Bill and Red fired. Bill fired his .38 four times, and Red fired three times. Tom Miller ran out the door, and as he did, Bachman blasted his automatic six times. Even though Clint had been hurt bad, he managed to hit Bill with a pair of brass knuckles, breaking Bill's jaw. Tom Miller fell back into the room. He had been hit behind the right ear. One bullet hit Clint in the upper left arm, grazed the bone, passed into his body, and lodged against the spine. Both Millers died within four hours. In spite of all the firing, each man had been hit but one time. The police later accounted for thirteen shots having been fired during the melee. Johnny Bachman never stopped to determine the results of the shooting, but went out the back door, sprinted up the alley, and drove away, leaving his Uncle Bill and Red to get away the best they could.

Red was apparently still in command of the situation and tried to get Bill up off the floor. However, he was out cold; and Red, not knowing that Bachman had taken a powder, went out to get him to help with Bill. It was then that Red saw that the car was gone. He looked back, saw Bill staggering up the alley, and went back to help him. Red took Bill's gun out of his hand, put it inside his shirt, and walked the injured Bill La Trasse about four blocks, when they were accosted by four police officers who had been notified of the robbery and shooting. The two men were searched and arrested.

According to Red, it was 1 A.M. on August 1, 1942, when he and Bill were taken to the city jail in Parsons, Kansas. One hour later, Sheriff Dense and Deputy Sheriff Crisswell, accompanied by a police escort, moved the men from Parsons and took them to the Montgomery County jail in Independence, Kansas.

When they reached the jail, they were separated and held incommunicado for four and one-half months while waiting arraignment, preliminary hearing, and trial. Both men refused to implicate Bachman. Their story was that they had used crooked dice and won all the money in Magner's dice game, and that the killings were the result of a fight over the money—that it was not a heist. They claimed that there was no third man. No one had actually seen Bachman. Just his shots from the hallway had been heard. Because Bill and Red refused to name him, it took the police three months to arrest him. When he was arrested, he immediately confessed to being a party to the robbery and killings during the commission of robbery. In Kansas the death penalty could have been inflicted in a case of this kind. What is the cost of freedom? In this case it was the money to hire the right lawyer for Bachman. Whatever defense Bill and Red might have had was now gone because of Bachman's confession. And when he agreed to testify for the state, the last slim hope went down the drain. Red and Bill realized that their only chance to escape the gallows was to try and bargain with the prosecution for a life sentence.

After considerable discussion, the deal was made. However, after the guilty plea was entered, the prosecution expressed a desire to delay sentencing until Bachman could be sentenced with them. This plan backfired when Bachman refused to plead guilty. His father hired the well-known criminal lawyer Joe Brady to defend the boy, and a trial date was set.

According to Red, "Glen Jones, the young and not too experienced county attorney, realized the weakness of his case against Bachman without the testimony of Bill and myself. He had nothing at all except Bachman's confession to link him with the case. Bachman had said that he threw his gun in the river. No autopsy was held on the bodies to determine the cause of death, or to establish whose bullet had killed whom. The prosecutor needed evidence and testimony, and the only ones who could furnish it was us. However, we turned a deaf ear to the proposal to turn state's evidence, in spite of the fact that we had every reason in the

world to feel bitter toward both Bachman and his lawyer, Joe
Brady.

"In 1922, at my trial for robbery, Joe Brady had been employed as a special prosecutor for the Banker's Association.
It was he who framed the evidence which resulted in my conviction. I had a score to settle with Joe Brady. I also had one
to settle with Johnny Bachman, for running off with the car
and for confessing when all he needed to do to beat the rap
was keep quiet. But instead, he spoiled every chance Bill and
I had. This could have been sweet revenge—just reprisal. But
neither Bill nor I would have anything to do with Bachman's
trial. Because of this, he was acquitted by the jury of the murder charge."

I have known Red Downs and Bill LaTrasse for many
years. In fact we were always very good friends. I have also
associated with and observed criminals of every type for many
years—more years than I care to think about. I have listened
to a myriad of case histories, alibis, arguments, and protests.
I have never listened to a more moving one than that told me
by Red of what happened to him while being held in the
"Blue Room" at the Independence jail in 1942. Had I heard
this story, even from Red, and not been fortunate enough to
observe him over the many years since that time, I think I
would have found it difficult to believe; but I have watched
him and lived with him and have seen the miraculous change
that has taken place, and I am absolutely sure that he did not
relate anything that was not true.

I have mentioned before that Red loved his mother very
much, in spite of his many misdeeds. When he was released
from Jefferson City, he vowed that he was through with crime
—that he would never do time again. He had already served
seventeen years in prison and was determined that this would
be the last time he would let his ailing mother down. He
really meant this. Consider, then, the spot he now found
himself in after just a brief period of freedom on parole. His

parole from the fifty-year sentence was broken, his invalid mother was left alone, and he was facing, at best, a life sentence. He was now forty years old, and it seemed doubtful that he could do the required amount of time on a life sentence and ever be free again. To Red Downs, this was IT. This was the end. He had missed the boat, failed completely and apparently definitely. The emotional impact of this realization was almost unbearable. The sands of time had run out; he wept bitterly.

According to Red's thinking at that time, there was nothing left for him in this world. There was only one thing to do— commit suicide. He wrote his mother a heartbreaking letter, asking her to forgive him his mistakes and for the pain and grief he had caused her. He told her that he realized the triteness of telling her he was sorry, but that he was, nevertheless. He tried in his own way to make her understand that he loved her. Then he prepared to die. Hanging, of course, would be the way—rope, bed, jump!

Before Red could carry out his self-destruction, fate intervened, as it has a peculiar way of doing. As if his mother had foreseen his intentions, she had mailed him a book on the subject of Truth. This seemed to be her last resort, her supreme attempt to voice her love and hope for her wayward son. There is an occult saying, often quoted in mystic circles, "When the student is ready, the teacher appears." The teacher in this case was Truth, and the forlorn and heartbroken Red was ready to accept it.

I feel sure that Red Downs did find his God, or his Truth. He also discovered that the suicide that he had contemplated was just as real now as if he had actually destroyed himself in body. He realized that his life had been but a series of lies, and that all that needed to be destroyed was his mixed up world and all the mistaken ideas he had had about it. The lies and the false world had to go.

For fourteen years after coming to Lansing, Harry made a

scientific study of metaphysics, the science of being. He pursued his studies with such books as the Old Testament; the New Testament; *The Science of Mind,* by Ernest Holmes; *The Rosacrucian Cosmo-Conception,* by Max Heindel; and Charles Fillmore's *Mysteries of Genesis and Mysteries of John,* as well as hundreds of other available books on Yoga and the historical religions. He kept his own counsel and seldom discussed his ideas and theories with anyone.

Red said that he had come up with a new concept which breaks down all barriers between races and religions. His intentions were to share his ideas with others upon his release from prison. When would that be? Well, it has happened. Red went out on parole January 16, 1967. At last reports, he is working and doing fine, and I predict that society will one day be proud of a man whom it once despised. He has what it takes to be a success in any field he chooses. He is a graduate of the Dale Carnegie courses and is a forceful speaker. He is a writer of no mean ability and is interested in helping the juveniles find the way to a life much different from his own.

The end to the Bill LaTrasse story is not so pleasant. After he and Red came to Lansing on the murder beef, Bill was destined to make the headlines twice more. While a patient in the prison hospital, Bill escaped over the wall one morning. As he fell free on the outside, he broke a hip bone. He crawled away in agony, and hid in an old shed near the prison. He remained there several days, but the pain became so intense that he was forced to call for help. He was returned to the prison hospital, where he remained almost constantly until he was released several years ago at the age of about seventy-four. Bill spent his last days with a sister in Denver, Colorado, and died there shortly after his release. This brought to an end one of the most exciting—and pitiful—careers in Kansas criminal history. The last of the lone train robbers had paid his debt to a society that he thought was hostile and unfair but toward which he felt no bitterness.

As this book deals mostly in the more-bizarre cases, it would be a terrible error of omission not to relate the story of the only gang of robbers who were true natives of Kansas and yet were never punished in this state, although death rode "the gale" for them all. This was the vicious, unscrupulous gang of cutthroats known as the Fleagles. This gang originated around Garden City, Kansas, in the Roaring Twenties, and made its debut into the big time at Ottawa, Kansas, on November 2, 1923.

Little Jake Fleagle, the field general of the gang, had served a short sentence in Oklahoma, and while doing so, had listened to the old-timers talk about bank robbery. He was a good listener, and when he returned to Kansas, he wasted no time telling "Ma" Fleagle what he had learned. Whether or not Ma was the brains behind the gang is purely a matter of opinion. However, it is fairly certain that she made no effort to discourage Jake and his gang.

The first recruit was Jake's big, lumbering, hard-eyed and trigger-happy brother, Ralph. Then the two enlisted George Abshier, a bootlegger from Colorado, and Herbert Royston, who tipped the scales at 230 pounds.

Ralph Fleagle had a weakness for guns and violence. He was the gang's official executioner, and according to reports, he did his job very efficiently and with real pleasure. The gang had pulled a few small jobs around their home vicinity, or were suspected of it, but the jobs were of so little importance that they were ignored. No one suspected that they were a vicious and ambitious gang, so they branched out into somewhat bigger things without anyone giving them much thought. The fact that they had been underestimated will become very apparent when it is learned what happened at Ottawa, Kansas, and from then on until the end.

The First National Bank of Ottawa had just opened on the morning of November 2, 1923, and a teller was making change for an employee of the Western Union Telegraph

Company, which was situated next-door to the bank, when several ridiculously costumed men exploded into the lobby and announced that a stickup was in progress. The men, wearing coveralls, high-peaked caps like those worn by railroad engineers, and red bandannas around their necks, scooped up a cool 150,000 dollars and went out a side door. A local painter who was working outside saw them and laughingly remarked that the way everyone was hurrying, a person would think a bank robbery was in progress. He little knew how close he came to being shot to pieces for that remark, but he probably knew a few minutes later and took the rest of the day off to celebrate his good fortune.

The alarm was quickly sounded, and the police began a systematic search. Roadblocks were set up, and every citizen was asked to report any suspicious-looking cars or characters. The route taken was known, but after the getaway car passed over a bridge, all traces of it were lost. A careful watch was maintained for days, but no signs of the robbers were ever found. It was discovered later that they had driven to an old, abandoned barn and had just waited until the heat was off, then had gone on about their business. No clues were found that would identify the men, and for the next five years the Fleagle gang operated without being given serious thought. When someone would mention the Fleagles, it was laughed off. These people were thought of as stupid and meek and were not considered seriously as suspects.

On May 23, 1928, at Lamar, Colorado, the gang ran into difficulties when they were met with resistance from the stubborn bank president of the First National Bank. The seventy-five-year-old bank official drew a revolver and shot Royston through the jaw. Then the old man, A. N. Parrish, and his son John were killed. This was the beginning of Waterloo for the killer gang.

With 218,000 dollars and two hostages, Everrett Kessinger and E. A. Lundgren, bank tellers, the bandits engaged the county sheriff in a hot gun battle and made their escape. They later dumped Lundgren out of the car, but forced Kessinger to go with them. A few days later, Dr. W. W. Winninger was kidnapped from his home near Dighton, Kansas, and forced to administer to Royston, after which he was killed and left in a ditch in his wrecked car. Then, no longer having any use for Kessinger, they murdered him and left his body in a deserted building near Liberal, Kansas.

Feelings ran high over the killings, and the rewards totaled 42,000 dollars. Fingerprints found on Kessinger's abandoned car led to the capture of Ralph Fleagle, Royston, and Abshier. Little Jake had so far eluded his pursuers. The three men were tried, convicted, and sentenced to hang; and while they awaited their date with the hangman, the search continued for Jake. He was finally trapped at Branson, Missouri, mainly through the efforts of Joe Anderson, a much-feared Kansas police officer. Jake resisted and was shot to death.

When Ralph Fleagle approached the gallows at Canon City Penitentiary, it was reported that he looked the instrument of death over carefully, shook his head, and said, "This is sure gonna teach me a lesson."

The Ray Majors gang of bank robbers operated in Kansas, but its members were not actually native Kansans. However, it was in Kansas that they met their end, tragically and permanently. While in the process of leaving a bank after a robbery, the heretofore steel nerves of the leader, Ray Majors, apparently cracked. He was following an accomplice, Frank Lang, from the bank when he accidentally pulled the trigger on the shotgun he was carrying, almost blowing Lang's legs off. They managed to get into the getaway car, where Frank Lang deliberately shot Majors with a hand gun. The bullet lodged against his spine, paralyzing him from the waste down. Ray and another of the gang were captured shortly after, and it was reported that Ray had been fingered by a member of his gang because he was a burden. He was brought to the hospital at the Kansas State Penitentiary. Lang was later apprehended, but did not arrive at the prison until after Majors had died. Lang served six years for bank robbery and then was paroled.

Another big robbery, which involved two former police officers, was the robbery of a Santa Fe payroll from a messenger of the Merchants National Bank in Topeka. This robbery took place directly across the street from my home, and while I did not witness it, I knew the participants well. George Probasco had been one of Topeka's top detectives for many years. He had left the police department and set up a private detective agency. His office was next to the bank in question, and he planned the robbery. He checked the date, the time, and the route of the messenger for several months, and at the same time he was busy recruiting men to do the job. He picked another ex-policeman, Eugene Leach, as his lieutenant, and a man named Pruitt and one whom I scarcely knew. He approached me several times; and although I didn't know at the time just what he had in mind, I knew it was a robbery, and I declined because I could not trust an ex-policeman.

On the appointed day, Leach and Pruitt parked in their car on East Fifth Street near the alley, and the other man stood on the corner across from the bank, where he could see George Probasco in his office window. When the messenger came out and got into his car, George gave the signal to the man on the corner, who in turn fingered the car to Leach and Pruitt as it passed him. When the car got past the gunmen, they pulled in behind it and followed it until it almost reached Monroe Street, a block and a half away. Then they crowded it and forced the messenger to turn south on Monroe and into the curb. They took the payroll of 17,500 dollars without any trouble and drove away. It is not known how the police got the information that tied Probasco and Leach into the deal, but the general consensus among the underworld characters was that Probasco intended to make a hero of himself and snare the entire loot for himself by naming Leach, knowing that Leach would sing on the other two men—and Probasco. But George figured that if he did the fingering, he could say that Leach and the others were only trying to pin him for detecting their job. It didn't work out that way. Both Probasco and Leach were arrested and charged.

Both of these men immediately named the dupes, and all were in custody. However, Probasco made bond, and Leach was put in what was called the twin cell of the Shawnee County Jail. This cell looked out on an alley and over some backyards of Van Buren Street. It was lined with old sheds. One night, while Leach was walking back and forth in his cell, a shot from a rifle was fired from one of these sheds, but it missed. George Probasco was suspected, but it was never proven against him. He had dealt only with Leach, and no one else could testify against him. If Leach were dead, there would be no way that Probasco could be convicted.

All four men were convicted of robbery and sent to Lansing. I later talked with George, and while he didn't say that he fired the shot at Leach, he did say something that left no doubt in my mind. We were talking one day about the case, and he said, "I muffed my best shot."

One of the more notable alumni of KSP was Alvin "Creepy" Karpis, who was a federal prisoner at McNeil Island Penitentiary from 1934 until his release in 1969. He had been convicted of participation in the kidnapping of William Hamm, a wealthy St. Paul, Minnesota, brewery owner. I knew Alvin when he was a little fellow, and I find that I cannot accept many of the disparaging things said about him. He has been described—most likely by some reporter who never saw him—as a mean-looking, pasty-faced kid. I was always interested in Al as a human being, and I know for a fact that he possessed, in addition to his criminal tendencies, a compassionate feeling for others who were in less favorable situations than he was himself. I found him to be a boy who was willing to listen to reason if he had confidence in the person who reasoned with him. Of course, it must be remembered that he was just a lad at that time. What changes took place in later years I cannot say. I can say that I firmly believe that I am partly responsible for the fact that Al never did become a drug addict—or if he did, I failed to hear about it, and I had regular reports on him.

It was customary for the young—and some of the older—thugs to hang out in a little shanty in the McCleery-Dudley coal yard on East Fourth Street in Topeka. I was older than most of these kids and was already a drug addict with an "oil-burning" habit. I used to go to this shanty to take a fix. Al hinted to me several times that he would like to try the stuff out. I gave him a lecture and told him if I ever caught him taking dope, I would kick his pants good. He apparently believed me. He promised me he never would, and I don't think he ever broke that promise.

It could be said that Alvin's destiny began to shape up after he met and became a close friend to Freddie Barker, one of the infamous "Ma" Barker's sons. Whether Alvin had known Freddie before they met at the Kansas State Penitentiary or not is a matter of mixed opinions. It is my belief that they first met after both had arrived to serve short sentences.

After both were released, they kept in close contact, and finally Alvin joined with the notorious family. Before this meeting, the Barkers were little more than a band of petty heisters and thieves, preying on small businesses and filling stations. However, prior to Alvin's enlistment with the family, Herman had done some fairly big jobs, including murder. Ma took an immediate liking to Alvin and recognized his ability to plan jobs and the means by which they should be handled. His uncanny shrewdness led to his being wooed by every big bandit gang in the country, and he planned many of the jobs performed by John Dillinger and others who would have been far less successful had they not had the brains of Alvin Karpis behind them.

Over the years I kept as close a watch on Alvin as was possible under the circumstances, and I know that he was hardly ever one of the executors of these jobs, but merely the guiding hand. I have read reports concerning his manning a machine gun at "Little Bohemia" the night an agent of the F.B.I. was slain. If, and only if, he found himself with no other means of escape, then he would have done this. Otherwise, he would not have—he was much too smart and cool-headed for such business. In fact, I have been told by men who were with him much of the time after I last saw him that Alvin seldom carried a gun. And he did not have one on his person when arrested in New Orleans, Louisiana, in 1936, according to newspaper reports, which also stated that the arrest was made by John Edgar Hoover himself—supplemented, according to these same papers, by forty or fifty agents situated on nearby rooftops, behind trees, and in hidden cars.

Alvin Karpis at this writing is sixty years of age and is employed as a clerk-typist for a social-welfare agency in Montreal, Canada, his home town. He has stated that he wants to live the rest of his years quietly and away from the limelight. He learned the clerk-typist work while imprisoned.

Alvin lived in Topeka, Kansas, as a boy, and attended Branner School, where he was a marble-shooting champion. He was a boy well liked by all who knew him.

My father was a blind man and used to spend a lot of time sitting on the old water plug that one time sat at Fourth and Quincy streets. Al knew my father and also knew that the old man liked hard candy. Every time he came uptown, Alvin would bring my father a bag of candy. They became fast friends. When at last the word got around that Alvin was a thief, my father refused to believe it. Even after Al became a nationally known criminal, my father would not believe the tales told about him.

If Alvin ever reads this, and I feel sure he will, he can be sure that one old blind man died believing in Alvin Karpis.

11

"Tennessee Tom"

The Warders strutted up and down,
And kept their herd of brutes, ...

A PRISONER in the Kansas State Penitentiary didn't always have to depend on time to get him out of prison—that is, if he had a little of the so-called root of all evil and a few connections. The records were all handled by inmates, and it was not a major project to persuade them to manipulate the records and bring about a man's release, providing he didn't have a life sentence or happen to be a prisoner of public interest. This program served for many years to help some convicts accumulate a lot of cash and put others on the "bricks" before their specified time.

This racket was practiced on a more or less limited scale for a long time. Only one or two men were used as solicitors. It was their job to locate and proposition the right men, those with money and some reputation for keeping their mouths shut. They collected the money, and the men in the office took care of the details. However, this became such a lucrative business that the operation was expanded, and at one time there were perhaps ten solicitors at work. This worked well and without any dire results until the ever-alert prosecutors began to notice that men they had sent down for ten years were reappearing on the streets. It did not take much of an investigation to discover what was happening, and the clamps were temporarily put on the deal.

The conniving convict, however, does not give up easily. And it was only a short while before another plan was put into operation. At that time the miners received two days good time and fifty cents for every ton of coal over their set task. Certain clerks at the mine top got together with the clerks in the record office, and a merger was arranged. This new one worked better—and faster—than the first plan had.

It was no big deal to steal a day here and a day there and put them to another man's credit. At first, this might not seem to amount to much. However, there were thousands of days involved each month, and it did not take long for them to add up. The men in the mine who had money could buy the days from another convict and have them added to his time. It was the overuse of this plan that resulted in the system of paying good time for coal being discontinued. Too many men were returning to freedom early, and this ended the good times—the bird's nest on the ground was destroyed. This slowed things down, but it did not stop the skullduggery. It has been said that the intelligence of men can produce no problem that the intelligence of man cannot solve. The record-keepers began to manufacture whole new sets of records for a client, and they set his release date for when he was able to pay for its being. This type of maneuvering could hardly happen today with the more-up-to-date records and methods, but it is likely that some fertile and agile mind is working on some plan that he thinks might work.

I have mentioned before the strange inclination of men to regard their freedom with disdain, of utter unimportance— until they have it taken from them. When this happens, they are willing to take any risk to regain it. Ususally these men choose the hard way to accomplish their mission, and many times they wind up crippled or dead—or with so much time that they can never hope to get out legally. The fellow who pulled the following caper was a shrewd and daring man in this respect.

He was an easy-going fellow who appeared to be rather dense and to have very little initiative. However, he was, in reality, dangerous and had escaped from many jails and prisons. He worked in the main dining room here. On this job he was out early and late and was counted several hours after the main count each day. He watched and he found that the night guard came in to work before the day man left, changed clothes, and left his uniform hanging in a locker. This was all he needed to know. He bided his time and made his plans.

The security measures in the prison during the late twenties and early thirties were haphazard, and it was not difficult for anyone wearing a uniform cap and blue suit to go out through the front gate. This man slipped in one evening just after the night guard had changed, put on his uniform, and walked through the gate without being challenged.

He was missed a few hours later. A thorough search was made of the surrounding countryside, but no trace of the escaped convict was found. It was learned later that he had rented a room nearby, waited for the heat to die down, then had gone on about his business. He was never returned to this prison, but he was apprehended, convicted, and executed in Kentucky for the murder of a policeman.

Security regulations have been strengthened over the years, and most of the crude attempts to escape which were used in the past would not get a good start now. Counts are more frequent and accurate, and precautions are taken to see that no prisoner has access to anything that would contribute to a successful escape attempt. Of course, men still do escape occasionally, and there will never be a time when they won't. But in addition to finding it harder to do so, an escapee finds it almost impossible to remain at large very long—in fact, it has become so hopeless that the smart convict would rather try the courts and other ways that are available to him than to take a chance that has so little promise of success.

Men have tried garbage cans, laundry bags, and sealed boxes as a means of gaining their freedom. Some have made it, but very few, considering the number of men who have passed through the prison since its beginning. A couple of daring men once stole a switch engine when it came inside the walls, and attempted to crash the gate. They might as well have tried to crack the Maginot Line with BB guns. All they got for their trouble was steam burns, a good working-over by the guards, and some more time.

All prisons have a goodly array of "jailhouse lawyers," and Lansing is no exception, except that perhaps those serving there are more versatile than most. It is possible to get a writ of "happus cappus," "hocus-pocus," or even "turn-me-loosem" for a small fee. Any one of these masters of jurisprudence will show you—in the law books—that "they can't do this to you." It just cannot be done, but they do not explain how you happen to be there, or how they happen to be there.

Seriously, it is amazing how much real talent in this field can be found in prison. Men who feel that their rights have been violated work hard and long searching the lawbooks for proof of their contentions, and some of the cases they present would probably cause the immortal Mr. Blackstone to raise his eyebrows in surprise. I sincerely believe that the legal profession may have lost some very fine talent to the criminal element when some of these men made the wrong choice. Had these men been encourage, permitted, or even persuaded at an early age to apply their knowledge—or capacity for knowledge—in the right channels, they might have contributed much to the society from which they have been cast out.

About the time that I entered the penitentiary in 1924, there was a man beginning his criminal career in the hills of Tennessee. He had become more or less a legend—and a nightmare—to many prison officials and police officers throughout the nation. This is his story, and it equals any true story in the annals of crime. It contains everything except murder. This man was not, and is not, vicious. However, he might be termed dangerous if crossed while in the commission of a crime. But I knew him as a loyal, honest, and well-liked prisoner. His name is John Harry Allen, alias "Tennessee Tom." While it would take more space than this book can possibly provide to tell his complete story, I will cover the highlights in order that the reader may be better able to understand how little things that are considered only mischievous can blossom into a life of crime.

John Harry Allen was born in Carroll County, Tennessee, on November 10, 1904. This was hill country, and young John, who will be referred to hereafter as "Tennessee Tom," was, like most hill folk, not an advocate of modern law and order. He began stealing and fighting at an early age, and he developed a hankering to see what was on "the other side of the hill." His neighbors, especially the law-abiding ones, did not try to discourage this idea; in fact, they thought it was a good one—for them.

In 1924, when Tom was twenty-one years old, he left his native hills and went to Arizona, where he became acquainted with a famous hunter by the name of Ben Lilly. He worked with this man for about six months, when again the wanderlust drove him to seek new pastures. He went to the Pacific Northwest and again became engaged in hunting. This time with "Cougar" Dave Lewis, a noted government hunter. Tom and Dave became fast friends, and the partnership lasted until 1928, when Tom decided to go to Pocatello, Idaho, for a visit. It was his intention to return to Dave and his hunting, but here fate intervened and started one of the most exciting and dramatic careers in the annals of American crime.

My notes do not tell me exactly what Tom got into at Pocatello, but I presume, knowing Tom as a dyed-in-the-wool gunman, that he heisted someone and relieved them of their earthly goods.

I will relate in detail one or two of Tom's miraculous escapes, but to explain them all would be more of a job than I care to tackle. Suffice it to say that he has escaped from more jails and prisons than the great Houdini did from straight jackets. Tom might well be termed the "Prince" of escape artists, as his record surpasses that of the touted Willie Sutton; and Tom's exploits would be great material for one of the television writers to toy with.

Tom made more escapes from the Kansas State Penitentiary than anyone knows about, except Tom and perhaps myself. In fact, he made three more than the records will show. He didn't get away any of these times, but he did get outside the walls. This is a rather weird story, but it is true, and those of us who were acquainted with the route Tom took can see that it is not far-fetched.

It is known that he left here one time in a tallow barrel, and one time over a cellhouse. However, long before either of these escapes, while working at the mine top, Tom pulled what he terms the prize bobble of his career. It was known that Tom was a tough man to keep in prison, and as a result, he was watched very closely. The boss of the mine top, Jimmy Nicholson, was not at all happy when Tom was sent to work for him. He said, "This guy is as slippery as an eel, and I would just as soon he worked somewhere else." It wasn't that he disliked Tom, he just didn't want the shuck* to fall on him when Tom turned up missing, which he was sure he would do.

Jimmy kept close tabs on Tom for a long while, in what he thought was a secret manner. What he didn't know was that Tom was also keeping a close tail on him. And when at last

* Blame.

Jimmy saw nothing but what seemed to be perfect behavior, Tom saw what he thought was a sure way out.

A small motor was used to push a big steel car from the mine top to the dump near the creek a few hundred yards away. This motor was driven by a trusty, and the trip was examined by a guard each time it passed the gate. Tom figured he could fix a place beneath the motor, ride it out, drop off at the dump, and be on his way. There was one problem—in fact, there was more than one, but Tom only noticed that there was a slot through which he could be seen by the guard if he looked carefully enough. In order to find out if the guard ever paid any attention to this slot, Tom pasted a piece of heavy brown paper over it, sprinkled it with dust, and waited. After several days had passed and the paper was unmolested, he knew he was safe on that score. So he fixed his nest and, at the appropriate time, crawled in.

The big car was loaded with slate and rocks, and the motor began its trip to the creek—and what Tom thought was his freedom. When the stop was made at the gate, Tom heard the guard give the go-ahead, and he felt the motor begin its move toward the creek. He was elated—he was sure that he had beaten the law again. The motor slowed and then stopped to dump the car. Tom looked down to where there should be a space which would allow him to slide out—and it wasn't there. The slate and debris had piled so high that it stood above the rails, and Tom could not get out.

When the motor got back inside the walls, Tom found that his troubles were not over. He couldn't get out inside either as long as the motorman was on the car. He made two more trips out before they called it a day and locked the motor up. When they did, Tom slipped out, and realizing he must have been missed, he quickly went down into the power plant, where a friend of his had a jug of hooch. He sprinkled himself with it, and then went hunting his boss, who was also hunting him.

He staggered a little as he drew near, and giggled as if he was tipsy. Jimmy sniffed, then said, "Tom, you're drunk. I've been looking all over the mine top for you."

Tom giggled again, and said, "Oh, I ain't drunk, boss, just had a couple of drinks—then I got sleepy and took a nap."

Jimmy looked him over, and replied, "Well, I won't report you this time, but don't do that again. I was about to turn in the alarm on you." Tom promised, and that ended the only escape of its kind to my knowledge. But it was typical of this will-o'-the-wisp, who was always able to get into more jams than a bushel of raspberries.

Tom has escaped from this prison several times, from Kilby prison in Alabama, and from the North Dakota prison. In addition to the fifty-one years he served at Lansing, he owes ninety-nine years in Oklahoma, thirty-five years in Alabama, and twenty-one years in North Dakota. However, North Dakota has since released him from their prison as discharged, because they saw no chance of ever getting him back.

Tom escaped from Kilby prison in Alabama in 1952, after serving thirteen months, and went to North Dakota, where he got a twenty-one-year sentence out of Fargo, North Dakota, for robbery. He stayed at Bismarck about long enough to get a shave and a haircut, and then left—by rail—for other parts. This escape, while not a masterpiece, was the result of very shrewd thinking and alertness on Tom's part, and perhaps some negligence on the part of the prison officials at Bismarck.

At that time, the prison at Bismarck used coal for its power, and the coal was shipped in by rail. Tom watched and saw that on a certain type of car there was a heavy steel stringer which ran beneath the car from end to end and that this stringer was hollow and left ample room for a man to hide. There was just one problem—he had to figure out how to get into the stringer, since it was solid at the bottom. Somehow Tom managed to get two planks in the floor of the car sawed and lifted out, then replaced after he had lowered himself into the hollow stringer. This was probably a job that had some inmate help, although Tom has not said, and I didn't ask. At any rate the car went out, and "Tennessee Tom" went with it. A few weeks later, while trying to locate a car which he could steal and drive back to Kansas, where he was about as welcome as a rattlesnake, he became involved in one of the really bizarre cases of crime. This caper became known as "Who Stole the Streeter Baby."

Tom was driving around with a friend near Streeter, North Dakota, in the friend's car. Tom was looking for just the right car to steal, one that was not too conspicuous, but sturdy. They located just what he thought he wanted. However, as it turned out, it was the last car on earth that he did want. It was parked near a church, and Tom told his pal to let him out and said that he would meet him near another house of worship about twenty miles away.

Tom got in the car and decided to drive around and try "his" new car out. He drove around the countryside, and then proceeded to the spot where he was to meet his friend. As he sat in the empty churchyard waiting the arrival of his accomplice, he happened to look toward the back seat, and he saw a bundle. He thought it was a coat or blanket, and for a few minutes gave it no thought. However, curiosity finally got the better of him, and he put a hand back and touched the bundle. His heart almost jumped out of his body—he had touched the warm face of a sleeping baby.

Tom is a man who does not excite easily, but this was an extreme case, and he was very perturbed. He made sure that the baby was safe from falling off the seat, then he went out to the road in front of the church to see if his friend was coming. When he didn't see him anywhere, he went back and turned on the car radio. His worst fears were confirmed. He was not only being sought for car theft, but also kidnapping. Road-blocks had been set up all over the area, and every citizen had been asked to keep a close lookout.

When the friend arrived, Tom told him what had happened, and his buddy told him to put the kid out and beat it. Tom said no to this. He was not going to let anything happen to that baby. It was cold, and the baby would freeze. He told his friend to go on home and to look for him when he saw him coming. He said he would take care of the baby.

Tom drove the side roads for about twenty miles, back toward the direction of Streeter. He saw a big orchard and figured he had better get off the roads until he could figure out what to do. He drove to the center of the orchard and parked. He saw a house in the distance. By then it was night, and he saw that the lights were on in one room. He made sure the baby was all right—it was still sound asleep—then he went toward the house. He crept up onto the back porch, eased open the screen door and fastened it back. This proved later to have been a good idea. He sneaked into the kitchen and listened. While he was there, the light went out, and he heard someone in an adjoining room.

As Tom left the kitchen he noticed a big sheepskin coat and a blanket on the porch. He grabbed both and made his way back to the car. As he walked across the bumpy orchard ground he thought what a queer trick fate had played on him. He was being hunted as a kidnapper, and how in the world could he ever make them believe it had been an accident. He had been in some tight spots before, but this one was the tightest of all.

When he arrived back at the car where the baby was still asleep, he carefully wrapped the little fellow in the sheepskin coat and blanket, made sure there was a place where air could get in, and began the trek back toward the farmhouse. He stepped lightly onto the porch and listened and listened. There was no sound coming from inside. He was glad now that he had fastened the screen door back. It would have been some trouble to open it with the large bundle in his arms. He just hoped now that the baby would continue to sleep. He stepped into the kitchen and stood still for a minute to make sure there was no activity in the living room. When he was satisfied that all was well, he slipped in and started to lay the bundle on a couch. He reconsidered this, however, realizing that the baby might fall off and be hurt. He put it on the floor, up against a wall, so that should anyone be walking around in the dark, he would not step on it.

As he lay the baby down, it stirred and whimpered for the first time. Tom hurriedly made sure the covering was all right and then took it on the lam out of there. He went up into the orchard and waited to see if the whimpering of the baby had awakened anyone. After about five minutes when no light showed, he decided that everything was all right and made his way back to the car.

Once back at the vehicle, he decided he had better abandon it and walk. If he was caught with the car, he was a cinch for a kidnapping charge and had a good chance of being lynched. He couldn't see any use in risking that. He began walking toward his friend's home, and after stumbling through the night, he arrived at his destination early next morning. He listened to the radio and read the papers, and while he was contemplating how to get out of the country, he was astounded at the report just coming in on the radio. The baby had been found. It was in good health and apparently happy. The folks in the farmhouse did not wake up until their own children, who had been to a late movie in town, came home and found the baby. They immediately recognized the child, because—well, here is the strange part of the drama—Tom had, by a strange coincidence, picked the house of the baby's cousin to leave it in. This fact was almost enough, on top of what had already happened, to drive Tom to the laughing academy. This was fate at its fickle best.

It is not known whether the truth was ever learned at Streeter, but if not, there is no longer any doubt about "Who Stole the Baby."

In an article entitled "FBI Lab Protects Innocent," by Joe Henderson of the Kansas City *Times* and *Star* staff, there is a reference to John Harry Allen, alias Tennessee Tom:

. . . As important as improved scientific techniques are in modern crime detection, the "man behind the microscope" is equally valuable. The "man" was particularly important in the apprehension of John Harry Allen, a member of the FBI's exclusive "Top Ten" fugitive list. Allen had escaped from prisons in four states, including the Kansas state prison at Lansing. He completed his second escape from that institution by hiding in a tallow barrel which was loaded on a delivery truck and hauled out.

Within the next month, supermarkets were held up in Enid, Oklahoma, and Des Moines, Iowa, by a gunman who handed the store manager a holdup note. The notes were forwarded to the FBI lab where a perceptive technician observed a striking resemblance between the handwriting on the notes and a letter written to a newspaper a few years back in another, unrelated case.

Further investigation showed that the letter to the newspaper and the two holdup notes were written by the same man—and that man was John Harry Allen. The lab report went to the police at Enid and Des Moines identifying the writer of the notes as Allen. Within a few weeks he was arrested in Bartlesville, Oklahoma . . . .

The report went on to say, "barring an escape, he is slated . . ." —but he did escape.

At this writing, Tom is in Lansing and has received some consideration from the board of pardons. He is scheduled to see a parole board soon, and he hopes to be returned to either Oklahoma or Alabama so that he can try and get something done in those states in order that he might enjoy the rest of his life a free man. I talked with Tom recently, and while he did not tell me of his future plans, he seems to have mellowed with age and exhibits a rather strong desire to try living on the level. I wouldn't say that the probability of Tom's moral rejuvenation merits great odds, but I do believe an even bet might be safe.

Tom is a poet of no mean ability—his work reflects his somewhat nonchalant attitude and quaint, to say the least, philosophy. I think it might be well at this point to present a few lines of Tom's work called "If There Is No Wind—Row."

> Since that day back in twenty-four,
> Many's the mile I've strayed
>   From my Dixie home,
> In the hills of Tennessee.
>   And like many another lad
> With bold adventures in his blood,
>   I sallied forth to roam strange lands
> And sail the Seven Seas
>   In quest of adventure, fame and fortune.
>   At an age very young,
> Bread and butter I found hard to earn,
>   For an easy way I turned to the gun
> And my way since I've paid
>   With loot from my six-guns.

And so, this is but a glimpse into the fantastic and exciting past of a boy who left his native hills to become a notorious outlaw, as so many others like him did in the long ago. It would seem to me that by virtue of the many daring escapes made by this man, according to the records and his own admission, his career serves to dim somewhat the brilliance surrounding other characters who have won national recognition.

Tom is still alert and physically sturdy. Although he is a bit grey and a little less active, his blue eyes still twinkle with his smile and Tom is in no sense bitter about his life's misfortunes. He realizes that he is the only one who can be blamed.

12

---◆◆◆◆◆---

Rehabilitation—
The Kansas State
Penitentiary Today

For each man kills the thing he loves
Yet each man does not die.

Up to this point you have been given a view of the prison of
the past—its horrors, mistakes, and the reluctance of society to
demand reform. We have reviewed the malpractices which
served only to aggravate the already twisted attitudes of men
who erred because they had never been taught the art of living as respectable human beings.

The prison of today is a far cry from the one of yesteryear,
but very few people, especially the prisoners of today, appreciate this fact, because they did not know the place at its
shameful worst. To the prisoners, the very fact that they are
incarcerated and are required to obey the rules is but a con-
tinuance of prison procedures from hundreds of years ago.
After reading about the old prison and its inhabitants, and
then being reminded of the conveniences and attitudes of today, it should be easy to see that both society and the criminal
have begun to realize their mistakes and are determined to do
something about them. They are beginning to face the problem with understanding and a willingness to bend a little.

213

This is the only way any appreciable progress toward curtailing crime can be made.

The brutalities and the tortures of the past are no more. They have been replaced by punishments that tend to impress the offender with the fact that he must learn to accept authority and learn to live in accord with the concepts of his environment. In place of the rock pile and holes of filth and hunger, a man who errs is sent to a new and modern building known as the Adjustment and Treatment Center, where he is treated in such a manner that he can and does concentrate on his behavior, and not on when he will get another meal or get his head beaten nearly to a pulp.

Do not get the idea that I am trying to say that prison today is "peaches and cream." It is far from that, and always will be. No prison will ever be peaches with or without cream—prisons will always be hell. There are so many improvements yet to be made that the men who are conducting the effort hardly know where to start; but slowly they are making progress—in fact, great strides—and the key to it all is rehabilitation.

Just as what has gone before may seem unbelievable to those who have never been in prison, so the prisons of today would seem unbelievable to the prisoners of yesteryear. They would find it hard to believe that men are no longer beaten and exposed to brutal and uncivilized punishments. They would doubt the fact that we have food that can be compared with that of a good restaurant outside and that it is not so putrid as to cause those near it to be nauseated.

When a man violates the rules now, he is sent to the modern and comfortable Adjustment and Treatment Center, where he is allowed a cell by himself and has the same privileges accorded other men except that he cannot go out at will. He has a soft mattress and a pillow, with sheets and pillow case. He receives the same food that is served in the dining room. He is counseled, not beaten and tortured, and when he shows signs of having changed his attitude, he is returned to the population and given another chance. Tobacco and newspapers are permitted, and each cell has radio earphones. And all this is proving, not only to the prisoner, but also to the officials, that punishment such as was meted out for many years was never the answer.

The old, dark, foul-smelling mess hall is no longer at Lansing. The narrow tables which faced in one direction are gone, and in their place are small metal tables of pastel colors which seat four men. A man may now choose his eating companions, and there is an air of cheerfulness in the air-conditioned, well-lighted dining room. Since these changes have been made, it has become apparent that environment and appearance have a great influence on the appetite. It is reported that food consumption has increased sharpely since this new system has been in effect.

Several months ago I was privileged to attend a Dale Carnegie graduation class. After the ceremonies a luncheon was held in the dining room. I was amazed to see visitors from outside—men and women—sitting at the tables with the prisoners and having a wonderful time. I spent most of the very enjoyable evening reminiscing—wondering what some of my old convict friends would say if they could see what I was seeing. I know they just could not believe it unless they did see it—and even then it would be a difficult thing to accept. I know I would never have believed it if I had not seen it.

In contrast to the old days, when I had to struggle to educate myself, I do not hesitate to say that today this prison boasts one of the finest, most complete educational systems in the United States. Regardless of his crime or social background, a man can enroll and receive the same attention that any other man gets. Classes range from those for beginners to the college level. A man can get a bona-fide high school diploma, and it is possible to earn as many as thirty college credits by correspondence. The textbook library is crammed with books covering almost any subject, and these can be checked out as needed by either pupil or non-pupil.

These are just a few of the things that have happened in recent years, and they would certainly astound the prisoners and officials who were here long ago. But this is just the beginning of a new era, a new look in prison administration, for which we can thank an aggressive penal director and warden. It is the beginning of an age that will, if continued, see "The Devil's Front Porch" become more like a training center aimed at producing capable, law-abiding men and women instead of completing their destruction and adding them to the "Legions of the Lost."

A fine sports program is a part of the new setup, and it is one to be proud of. On the yard are miniature golf courses, weight-lifting equipment, and horseshoes. In addition to a varsity baseball team, there are many sandlot teams, and softball is well represented. The varsity teams are permitted to go out and play other teams—in fact, they belong to leagues. In 1968 and 1969 the varsity teams participated in the regional play-offs of the National Semi-Pro Tournament in Wichita and gave good account of themselves, even though they did not win a national spot.

I am not well enough acquainted with basketball and football to judge what our teams can do, but I do know that they give their all for old KSP just as they would for a college outside. And from what I have been told, these teams might even give some of the college teams a rough go.

These things, along with a religious program which presents one of the fine religious choirs in the country, are proof of the sincerity of the men in command of our prison system, and of their efforts to make the system pay dividends in human character. It is a bit early to judge with any degree of accuracy just how much this will affect the overall problem—only time will tell that. But it is certain that it will have some effect; and that is much more than could ever be said for the system as we knew it forty years ago.

While the vocational-training project has not yet come close to its potential, it promises to play a big part in future operations. The reason it is not more advanced at this time is because of the space problem and the fact that the public has long been reluctant to get solidly behind such a program. However, in recent months, more and more influential people are becoming interested, including such large firms as Philco and others of equal stature. These companies realize the potential of the men they find in prisons, who have, for the most part, become entangled with the law because of inadequate training and education. These companies apparently are willing to take a chance on these men, believing that most of them do want to live more useful and happier lives. In realizing this and helping them, they are not only doing the prisoner a favor, they are also lightening the load for the taxpayer and gaining for themselves men who may prove valuable to them in the future. There can be no doubt that everyone concerned profits when all try to see the problem as it really is and want to do something about it.

I recently talked with Warden S. H. Crouse, and while he did not reveal any of his ideas to me—which is understandable —I gathered from his conversation that he has far-reaching plans for the betterment of the prison. I was impressed with his sincerity, and I noted that he is a cautious man with a good understanding of the prison's needs. I believe he is very well equipped for his important position and is not easily misled.

The warden pointed out that in the past, the main reason why so many things that were started failed to get finished was because usually the warden stayed in office just long enough to make plans and get the ball rolling, then was replaced because of politics. I know this to be true. I served in Lansing under several wardens—at least six, and some of them twice— before coming under Mr. Crouse. Until this time, when a new governor was elected, we could almost certainly look for a new warden. This practice did more to prevent improvements in the prison than all the others combined. It usually took a new warden a year or more to find out just what was needed. Then it took another year or more to get the necessary backing. About the time he was in position to start his project—a new governor, a new warden. When this happened, the whole thing had to be done again. It became a vicious circle, and nothing could be accomplished.

I do not hesitate to say that I have noticed more improvements and more real interest shown in the prison and the prisoners in the last three years than I saw in the other forty. Interest is shown not only while they are here, but also after they leave. There are two very fine programs underway here now to help men get jobs—and training for jobs. These are the Seventh Step Foundation and a vocational-counseling program sponsored by the State of Kansas and the United States government. I cannot help but believe that if given the proper support, the present penal administration will make history that all Kansans may be proud of—just as we are of the progress made in mental health. This progress will be slow. It always is in cases of this kind. However, the indications are that patience and faith will pay dividends before too long.

We must keep in mind that it took hundreds of years for our penal system to get into the deplorable condition it was in, and it will take considerable time for it to be repaired. It has in the past been a political football, and the watchword was "We got 'em in, now all we gotta do is keep 'em in." If there were no internal troubles and the records showed that a profit was being made, they were content to let things ride. No thought was given to the possibility that men could be made into better men. The law was only interested in getting its "pound of flesh" and producing a good public image. They failed to see that to treat men as they were treated, and then someday have to turn them back into society, was foolish, if not insane.

Most men were here because of some real or fancied injustice on the part of someone, or because they did not know how to do any different than they did. When they were mistreated, they made up their minds that when they got out, someone was going to have to pay for it. This went on for years, until the number of these bitter men grew into such a large army that society and its pitifully small law forces were never able to catch up with the odds. Whether anyone else realizes it or not, I know that had the criminals organized not so many years ago, officers of the law would have been so hopelessly outnumbered that they would never have been able to stem the tide, then—or ever. And mainly because the penal systems had been using the wrong methods for so long. The logic of this can be seen when we look at the progress being made now by using sensible and humane methods.

It is reported that crime is on the increase, and this is probably true. However, it should be taken into consideration that in this rapidly progressing world, new problems arise each day with which the average citizen is not able to cope. It should be recognized also that in compiling these statistics, many offenses which are not really crimes are included. Whether we care to admit it or not, it behooves the law-enforcement agencies to make the situation look as hopeless as they possibly can, for both financial and political reasons. If crime is on the increase—and I don't deny that it is—then it does not speak well for the methods used in the past. This alone should call for closer scrutiny of the laws in an effort to categorize the various crimes, and then establishment of agencies with trained personnel to combat them scientifically and earnestly.

Among the fine programs which are comparatively new here is Alcoholics Anonymous. It is one of the strongest and best-attended programs in the prison and speaks well for War-

den Crouse and his staff, as do the many other prisoner-better-
ment programs which have become reality under this capable
and sincere man's direction. The statistics show that the rate
of recidivism among the members is very low, and if only one
is helped to find his way out of his alcoholic problems, the
program is well worth the effort. And many men are in prison simply because they could not cope with this problem.

The Dale Carnegie Foundation holds classes here in human
relations and public speaking. This is a fourteen-week course,
and it is amazing what it does for most men who avail themselves of its offerings. The civilian instructors are dedicated
men who give freely of their time and knowledge to help prisoners find their mark in a free and sometimes frustrating
world. They learn to think on their feet and to do it construc-
tively. It teaches men how to get along with other people, and
this is one of the things most needed by the majority of criminals and potential criminals. This program, too, is a tribute
to the officials. It shows that they are truly interested in helping their charges to prepare themselves for the inevitable trip
back into the world of living people—to a new life, not just
another miserable existence. Mention should be made, and
with great appreciation, to the local leaders of this course for
their untiring efforts, namely, Gerald Abbott, Dan Adams,
and Ursel Gordon.

I have seen men who have graduated from this course go
out and make good on jobs which they would not have dared
to accept before. I have seen men who for years had been
withdrawn—almost antisocial—do a complete turnaround after finishing this course. I know this, because I was one of
them. And in view of what it did for me and others like me, I
know that it would be profitable for anyone anywhere to investigate this group.

It has only been recently that outside theatrical and musical
groups have been permitted to entertain here, and from all
indications this will continue as long as the men behave as

they have to date. One lady performer made the remark that she had been treated with more courtesy here than in many public places outside. Such observations as this help to dispel the mistaken belief that all prison inmates are ogres and morons, an image that is a holdover from the barbaric days that are gone forever from the prison system.

It is only fair that I emphasize the fact that both the officials and the inmates are to be commended for these improvements —it shows real effort on the part of the officials, and appreciation and cooperation on the part of the inmates. Any measure of respectibility gained for the system by these efforts can be attributed to sincerity on both sides.

The efficiency of any school can only be measured by the accomplishments of the students it produces, not the attractive curriculum it offers on paper or the social standing of its faculty. A prison can be, and should be, judged by the same standards—the accomplishments of the men it sends back to society. Every man who leaves a prison and succeeds is a living monument to those who helped him find his way back to respectability. It matters not how many dollars he earned for, or cost, the state, or how he affected the taxpayer. The final analysis can only be made by what he does after he leaves prison—what useful things he contributes to mankind.

The fact that he was a bum or a rogue before coming to prison, or that he was raised in shanty town, does not necessarily figure in the final summing-up. It is what he is now— not what he was. This, I believe, is what the penologists and society are learning; and they are getting better results by basing their treatment on this knowledge.

A program which promises to be of assistance in the rehabilitation of prisoners and is another example of the farsightedness of Penal Director Charles McAtee and Warden Sherman Crouse, is known as the Seventh Step Foundation. If statistics mean anything, the program has, during its six years of existence, proven the judgment of these authorities to be sound.

The program inside the walls is administered by a convict committee which conducts group discussion meetings every Monday evening. Outside guests are permitted to attend the sessions and participate in the discussions. The guests—business and professional leaders—have been invaluable resources for employing the men when they leave prison. As this interest has increased, more and more jobs have become available for class members, all of whom are within 120 days of their release dates. However, it was soon discovered that job offers alone would not meet the needs of some men, and what it known as the "man-to-man" plan was developed. This is a plan in which a "square John" who is financially able signs an agreement to accept responsibility for a released man's immediate needs (work clothes, a place to stay, etc.) until he is able to support himself. The amount varies from fifty dollars to one hundred dollars and is to be repaid by the ex-con as soon as he is self-supporting and able. His sponsor is not permitted to sponsor another man until he has been repaid whatever amount he had advanced to the man he is currently sponsoring. The real value in this man-to-man sponsorship plan is not the financial aid the sponsor agrees to give, but the friendship that many men coming out of prison have never had before. It is a very healthy relationship.

In the prerelease class sessions, conducted by the committee, group discussions focus attention on the Seven Steps and their application in the lives of class members. An effort is made to encourage each man to face up to the truth about himself and the world around him, to evaluate his strengths and weaknesses, to overcome his resentments, and to make realistic plans for maintaining his freedom and successfully integrating into society.

As the prerelease class enrollment grew larger, it was decided to enlarge the committe to eight men. The qualifications for men being considered for the committee are: They must show a sincere desire to improve themselves and prepare for their eventual return to society, with a view to maintaining their freedom once it has been obtained. They must be well known and respected by the inmate population and must show evidences of sincere effort toward rehabilitating themselves. The men on the committee do not have "out-dates" as the class members do. Most of the committeemen are two- to four-time losers who are presently serving long terms, ranging from fifteen to thirty years. This is in order that the committeemen might not be inclined to exert more effort toward favorable parole-board action, and less in helping the members.

It should be mentioned that the jobs and sponsors which the prerelease program of the Foundation offers do not constitute the primary purpose of the program as a whole. These are simply some of the fringe benefits. The primary purpose of the program is to help men straighten out their thinking, to motivate them with a desire to maintain their freedom, and to instill confidence in each man that he can do so.

The Reverend Jim Post said recently in a speech to the Jaycees of Kansas City that it was something how little knowledge people have about prison, in spite of the fact that they are the ones who are paying taxes to operate it. He said, "You should be concerned, because it costs you approximately $1,500 per man per year." And he added, "We are dealing with human beings down there. Everyone down there didn't plan to be there. We might as well get used to seeing ex-convicts, because 95 percent will be back on the street someday. All an ex-con is, is someone who has been punished— someone who has paid his debt to society."

In speaking directly of the prerelease program, the chaplain said, "It is estimated that the average practicing criminal is going to involve himself in at least ten major crimes before he is apprehended. If we take the 251 graduates of the program who haven't failed, and multiply this by ten, we have 2,500 crimes which weren't committed. And, if we multiply this same number of free men by the $1,500-per-year cost per man to the state for keeping them in prison, we have a $376,000 saving to Kansas. This should interest those who are more interested in the cost in dollars rather than the savings in human lives."

The Seventh Step Foundation has experienced a somewhat stormy history, due in part to controversy which has surrounded some of its early founders, and also due to the resistance shown by some local and state officials to innovations which threaten old ways of doing business. But the Foundation has survived. It continues to help convicts inside the walls and ex-convicts on the street; and with time-proven former inmates working shoulder to shoulder with respected community leaders, there is every reason to believe the organization will do important work in the future.

There are other programs just getting under way that will prove to be of great value to all concerned as time goes by. And I am sure that the heads of our system are not through searching for means by which to bring about greater results.

Within a few days I will leave "The Devil's Front Porch," and I will not return again. Of this I am certain. Though I have spent a considerable portion of my life here, I will not miss the place, for a prison can never be a home-away-from-home. I am not the same man who first arrived here forty-five years ago. I hope I am a better man; in any case, I am a different one. Perhaps as prisons hopefully change for the better, those who remain here and those who are yet to come will learn in much less time than I—and the Bill LaTrasses, the Tennessee Toms, and the Red Downses—that each man actually builds his own prison and designs the height and expanse of its walls. There is an exoteric prison, and there is an esoteric prison. One may escape from the former, but freedom from the latter depends on scaling the walls of one's self.

List of
Nicknames

I have noticed in the past that many people have a curiosity about some of the rather strange nicknames applied to men in prison. Some of these were brought in to me, and others were tacked on for various reasons. It should be interesting for the reader to try and see if he or she can figure out what prompted some of these names. Some are obvious, and others will mislead most people. For instance, one would naturally think that a man dubbed Killer would be vicious. This one was one of the gentlest and best-liked men in the prison where he was serving. "Bones" would seem to indicate a thin man. This one was six-feet tall and weighed about 250 pounds. So try your luck.

Boot-Nose	Chief	Mousie
Jelly	Bad Understanding	Gray-Ghost
Dopey	Humpy	Pluto
3-D	Father Flanagan	Snipe
Bullet	Rusty	Chi
Two-Gun	Dusty	Grinder
Kidney-Foot	Bull-Moose	Paddle-Foot
Chesty	Black-Diamond	Mule-Head
Our Father	Pooch	Catfish
Slick	Shivvy	Canada Yellow
Whiskers	Iron-Jaw	Blue Pete
Preacher	Guzzler	Panther Man
Whip	Blue-Eagle	Hatchet-Face
Hips	Big-Nose	Cat-Man
Cockeye	The Bloke	Snake Doctor
Jumbo	Peanuts	Cool Breeze
Zeno	Bear-Tracks	Slats
Snuffy	Poor-Boy	Bad News

Mushmouth
Salty Dog
Long-Gone

Honest Jake
Gruesome Gus
Foot 'n a Half
Stingaree

Big Hat
Foots
Bodiddly

81717